THE FARMER'S WIFE
A True Story

FRIENDSHIP, MARYLAND, 1877

"ONE OF THE MOST REVOLTING MURDERS
IN THE ANNALS OF CRIME."

The Baltimore Sun • DECEMBER 22, 1877

THE FARMER'S WIFE

A True Story

by Carol McCabe Booker

New Bay Books

THE FARMER'S WIFE
by Carol McCabe Booker

Editor
Sandra Olivetti Martin
New Bay Books
Fairhaven, Maryland
NewBayBooks@gmail.com

Cover:
Photo collage by Suzanne Shelden. Engraved portrait of a woman from page 97, *WOMEN: A Pictorial Archive from Nineteenth-Century Sources, 488 Copyright-free Illustrations for Artists and Designers,* selected by Jim Harter, Dover Press. Combined with photo of Calvert County tobacco barns in field by Suzanne Shelden.

Interior design by Suzanne Shelden
Shelden Studios
Prince Frederick, Maryland
sheldenstudios@comcast.net

A Note on Type: Cover and section heads are set in Walden Font Type No. 2. The text font is ITC Bookman Std.

Library of Congress
Cataloging-in-Publication Data

ISBN 979-8-9882998-3-7

Printed in the United States of America
First Edition

DEDICATION

In memory of Sallie Johnson Norfolk.

She loved.

She trusted.

She was betrayed.

CONTENTS

INTRODUCTION

TILL DEATH DO US PART

It was 1877, a mere dozen years since the end of the Civil War, a time when Maryland's sentiments might be described as bipolar. Maryland had not seceded from the Union, but slavery was legal in the state, and many of its citizens wanted to preserve that status quo. Families and friends split on the issue, and brothers marched off in opposite directions to fight on both sides in a sad conflict. The states, particularly the southern and border states, including Maryland, were still recovering.

In the former Confederacy, this was a period known as Reconstruction, and 1877 was the year a president was elected on his promise to end Lincoln's surviving legacy. These were tumultuous times, from a contested presidential election to deadly weather extremes, a bloody railroad strike and the actions of national and local legislatures. Reporters in every state covered the news for avid readers, and Maryland historically had several very popular newspapers.

Yet a single story first reported in *The Baltimore Sun* captured headlines throughout most of the year across the country. It was a tale of betrayal. Some called it an atrocious breach of faith; a fiendish, brutal violation of trust. Others even called it "inhuman," with hints of demonic possession. It began in May with "one of the most revolting murders in the annals of crime." The victim was a young mother who went to her grave never knowing why, and perhaps not even seeing her cowardly executioner.

Steadily and in excruciating detail, nationally syndicated reports illuminated a cold-blooded crime more chilling than the past winter's paralyzing frosts on the Chesapeake Bay. No detail was spared.

1

1877: A BONE-CHILLING BEGINNING

When the waters become hard as stone,
and the face of the deep is frozen.
—Job 38:30

On January 5, 1877, Baltimore's meteorologists recorded the city's lowest temperature: 1 degree Fahrenheit. The high temperature the day before had been just 21 degrees. But that was not the winter's worst, or even the actual temperature on the windswept and icebound Chesapeake Bay, which by the new year was frozen to crippling depths.

The freeze that began in mid-December with the decade's low of 27.3 degrees Fahrenheit now had watermen and lighthouse keepers alike imperiled by the ice. The Port of Baltimore was closed to traffic for several days while hundreds of ships hunkered down at Annapolis, waiting for meteorological relief. The thaw finally came at the end of the first week of the new year, when the temperature climbed to 38 degrees, and then crept up to 45, with a warm south wind and heavy downpours. But the worst effects of the freeze were still to come. The strong westerly winds that followed the thaw propelled numerous ice floes to the Bay's Eastern Shore, wreaking havoc in their path.

In Dorchester County, at the entrance to Tangier Island Sound, the Hooper Strait lighthouse was no match for the huge islands of ice that pounded its base. This was a screwpile lighthouse, one of about 40 positioned throughout the Bay after the Civil War to warn ships away from offshore shoals and sandbars. In these frigid winters, their spindly legs were like brittle sticks, vulnerable to shattering when battered by the enormous segments of pack ice that swept down the Bay toward the ocean during the inevitable thaw.

On January 11, an ice floe took the Hooper Strait lighthouse with it after shearing it off its pilings. Keeper John S. Cornwell and his assistant didn't wait to see where they might wind up. They grabbed a lifeboat, maneuvered it onto the ice, overturned it, and crawled beneath the hull. Nearly 24 hours later, frostbitten and weak after a night with only the boat for shelter from the freezing cold, they were rescued by a local waterman and taken to nearby Billy's Island, on the south side of the strait.

But there was no way to notify their families or the authorities that they were safe. It would be two weeks before anyone else knew what had become of them. Meanwhile, the ice swept the lighthouse about five miles south, where it sank up to its roof. Lighthouse tenders were eventually able to salvage its lens, lamp, and fog bell.

In mid-January, near the mouth of the South River at Annapolis, another drama was playing out. The keeper of the Thomas Point Shoals light, his assistant, and the assistant's wife were also struggling in the aftermath of the thaw that had weakened the ice and sent huge floes down the Bay. The running ice was shaking the two-year-old, six-sided Victorian cottage-style lighthouse so violently, the keeper reported, that the stoves had to be lashed down. At night, the ice breaking against the screwpile piers "sounded like the crackling of fire."

Then, on January 17, keeper Eugene Burchenal reported that the ice floes, some as much as two feet thick, had shaken the pilings so badly that the Fresnel lens was knocked over and broken into pieces. "Nothing," he wrote, "could stand that shaking up." Nevertheless, he advised his superiors he would try to stick to the house until further orders.

The light and its keepers survived.

Thomas Point Shoals Light, 1885.
(Photo by Major Jared Smith; National Archives)

RESCUES AND DISASTERS

Back on land, three oystermen showed up frostbitten and bedraggled at a police station in Baltimore with a nightmarish account. Their schooner had been frozen up in the ice at Eastern Bay, near Kent Narrows, with 70 or 80 other schooners and pungies (the two-masted oyster boats peculiar to the Bay). Their stock of provisions depleted with their last meal, a small piece of ship bread and coffee, the men started out walking across the ice. After a grueling day, they made it to the western shore, and then three days later to Baltimore, thanks to infrequent wagon rides.

They reported that 14 schooners had been driven ashore in a gale. Most of the vessels, having been laid up in the ice since New Year's Day, were out of provisions. Water was scarce, and many of the crewmen had frozen limbs. One man had drowned while trying to draw water through the ice. The city sent tugs down to Eastern Bay with food and other relief.

Two tugs had earlier tried to bring out of Eastern Bay a large fleet of oyster vessels that had been frozen in there for several weeks. The heavy drift ice proved too much for the initial tow of 14 schooners, and seven had to be cast loose. The ice then cut through four of those, requiring the tugs to abandon them after rescuing their crews. Three of the severed schooners sank out of sight, and another went down in just seven feet of water. Joined by a third tug, the convoy reached Annapolis safely with the surviving schooners and their crews, most of whom required medical care.

Reports such as these proliferated through January, not only in Maryland, but also up the Delaware River to Philadelphia and beyond to New York harbor. Newspapers described it as an "ice embargo" on the commerce of these Mid-Atlantic ports. Despite her nearness to salt water, the Statue of Liberty, just months into her reign over New York harbor, looked out on ice as thick as 15 inches in some places, and "solid as flint." Meanwhile, on the East River, thousands of daredevils reportedly ventured out to walk across the frozen six-tenths of a mile between the island of Manhattan and the borough of Brooklyn.

On the Chesapeake, oystermen defied the weather, insisting on plowing the Bay for the cash crop so much in demand up and down the East Coast. The oysters were plentiful, and the money better than ever. But in this kind of hard winter, the old saying was never truer: A man had to love it to do it.

The new year was off to a bone-chilling start. But not all the news around Southern Maryland during the winter of 1877 concerned the tragedies playing out on the Chesapeake. Other reports described some folks—especially the young—enjoying Jack Frost's antics. The *St. Mary's Beacon* reported, for example, that a daring young lady was the first to skate across the Patuxent from Trent Creek in St. Mary's County to Calvert County's Buzzard Point and back. Describing it as the first known passage between these two points, the paper advised, "only those who are acquainted with the nature of the stream here, can fully understand the danger incurred, and appreciate the feat of the adventurous." The reporter then cheekily described how a male companion had also tried it, and went through the ice to the "haunts and homes of Patuxent oysters," before quickly saving himself.

A WORLD APART

In the nation's capital, the new year started off with a grand reception hosted by President Ulysses S. Grant, who was counting down his weeks in the White House to the day when he would be succeeded by the winner of the November 7, 1876, election. The problem was that as of January 1, no one knew which of the two contenders for the position that would be. New York's Democratic governor, Samuel J. Tilden, beat Republican Ohio governor Rutherford B. Hayes in the popular vote by more than 260,000 ballots. But the electoral college tally was disputed amid allegations of electoral fraud, violence at the polls, and Black (predominantly Republican) voter suppression. There were even fears of another civil war. But neither that uncertainty nor a record snow storm interfered with the New Year's celebration at the White House. As reported in the *Calvert Journal* under the headline, "White House in a Blaze of Splendor"—

> *The New Year's reception of President Grant commenced today to one of the most severe snow storms ever known in this latitude. The snow began falling around 11 o'clock as the members of the diplomatic corps were assembling to pay their respects to the chief magistrate, and it continued throughout the day and into the night. The streets tonight are fully knee-deep with snow, and locomotion, either on foot or in vehicles of all descriptions, is a work of no little difficulty. Despite the terrible weather, however, arrangements for the reception were on a grand scale, and at the executive mansion there was a scene of revelry and animation that has not been eclipsed at any previous levee [formal reception].*

Besides the diplomatic corps, the gala was attended by the justices of the Supreme Court, members of the Senate and House of Representatives and officers of the Army and Navy.

Meanwhile, the two sides in the presidential election contest remained deadlocked at the end of January, when Congress created a bipartisan Electoral Commission composed of members of the House, the

Senate, and the Supreme Court to break the impasse before the end of President Grant's term at noon on March 4. The commission met that deadline shortly after 4 o'clock on the morning of March 2, when it declared Hayes the winner by a margin of one vote. The announcement came so late that the inaugural ball had been canceled due to the uncertainty of the outcome. Hayes was sworn in privately over the weekend, followed by a public ceremony on Monday, March 5, amid swirling snowflakes on the east steps of the Capitol.

About 30,000 people attended the 1877 Inauguration of President Rutherford B. Hayes on the east steps of the U. S. Capitol. (Library of Congress)

That evening, Hayes, outgoing President Grant and his cabinet viewed a massive, torch-light parade. Residents on both sides of Pennsylvania Avenue, from the Capitol to the White House, were asked to illuminate their homes, and the parade route was lined with calcium lights (known as "limelight"). Five thousand torches were also ordered for the procession, in which ten thousand men, mostly military, were expected to march.

In Southern Maryland, there was loud condemnation of the election results. Editorials in the *Calvert Journal*, the self-professed "Democratic in politics" weekly published in Prince Frederick, were vitriolic, calling the inauguration the "Drama of Fraud," and the new president the "epitome of all fraud." As for the Inaugural Parade, the paper proclaimed, "Never before upon the broad Avenue had there appeared a procession so sickening, so disgraceful." The editorial was accompanied by a Special Dispatch with a similar view:

> *The streets were alive with people, chiefly, however, the vilest dregs of Washington society....Washington has been since Saturday given completely over to the wildest of wild orgies, and no decent man can go upon the streets without being shocked and disgusted at the rampant viciousness which displays itself everywhere.*

Rutherford B. Hayes, 19th President of the United States.
(Library of Congress)

While never abandoning its position that Hayes' election was a fraud, over the ensuing year the newspaper softened its view of the man himself, giving him credit for steps to reform the government, and predicting that "we may indeed look for brighter and more prosperous days."

Besides Hayes' pledge to reform the government, part of the compromise reached by the two sides to resolve the disputed vote was the withdrawal of federal troops from southern states—the end, in other words, to the federal intervention that governed Reconstruction. Twelve years after the Civil War, the era of Reconstruction was coming to a close. By late fall, the newspaper had high praise for the President's "Southern pacification policy," calling it "so expressive of a genuine patriotism" that the editorial quoted the whole of it, including the new president's forward look to a time when:

> *a genuine love of our whole country, and of all that concerns true welfare, shall supplant the destructive forces of mutual animosity of races and of sectional hostility.*

OUT LIKE A LION

When spring finally tiptoed into Maryland, winter would not retreat without a fight. The low temperature at the northern tip of the Bay was only 12 degrees Fahrenheit on March 20, the day before the vernal equinox. Weather, however, even at record lows, was no longer the big newsmaker.

In Southern Maryland, two historic landmarks made headlines. One was the popular and once fashionable hotel at Point Lookout, at the confluence of the Chesapeake Bay and the Potomac River. Named for its role as a lookout for American forces during both the Revolution and the War of 1812, the scenic peninsula had been a resort for Baltimoreans before the Civil War, when it was turned into a Confederate prison-of-war camp. The hotel and many of the adjacent cottages, owned by a Philadelphia company, were destroyed by fire on March 16.

The other was Solomon's Island in the Patuxent River at the southern tip of Calvert County. The island had developed into a thriving destination at the midpoint of the Bay, after Delaware-born Isaac Solomon built what he proclaimed to be the world's largest oyster cannery. His 17 or more employees canned oysters in the winter and a variety of fruits and vegetables in summer. He had built dozens of homes on the island, attracting watermen and entrepreneurs to the approximately 70-acre site at the mouth of the river. And he donated land for the building of churches to meet their spiritual needs.

But something led the successful businessman to dissolve the oyster-canning company he had formed with his sons and allow the entire island to be placed on the auction block in 1875. The successful bidder was a Baltimore firm, the Permanent Building and Land Society, which plopped down $10,000 (considerably less than Solomon had poured into the island), and announced plans to create a summer resort, with cottages and a hotel. Now, two years later, they instead abandoned the venture, and the island was grabbed again—this time, like Point Lookout, by a Philadelphia company. Here, too, the plan was reportedly to convert the island into a summer resort, with accommodations designed to lure vacationers from Washington, D.C., as well as Baltimore. The local newspaper, the *Calvert Journal*, observed: "We know of no better location for that purpose, and believe that under proper management the Island, as a summer resort, would pay well." The sales price was either $12,500 or $15,000, depending on conflicting news reports.

The winter months of 1877 had seen challenges to which the residents of Southern Maryland, with its usually mild climate and ho-hum winters, were unaccustomed. But that was nature, and nature was unpredictable. Springtime, on the other hand, with its slowly warming temperatures and rarely any major storms, should have been a quiet transition to the upcoming summer on the Chesapeake Bay.

It was not. Especially not for residents of a mid-Bay community called Friendship.

2

AN UNFORGETTABLE SPRING

What potent blood hath modest May.

—Ralph Waldo Emerson

By early May, Maryland's oystermen were winding up a bountiful and profitable season. There was as yet no hint of the decline looming ahead in the final decade of the 19th century, a decline that would affect the livelihood of thousands of watermen.

But the state's economy was built on more than oysters. By 1850, according to the U.S. Census, tobacco was being grown in every county in Maryland, making the state second only to Virginia in production of the crop. In the former colonies around the Chesapeake Bay, tobacco was a major cash crop, especially in Calvert, Charles, St. Mary's, Anne Arundel, and Prince George's counties, where thousands of Marylanders preferred to plow the soil rather than the Bay.

For almost three centuries most tobacco cultivation —almost 900 man-hours of work per acre—was done by slaves. This reality was reflected in the demographics of the Southern Maryland counties, which at the end of the Civil War were predominantly Black.

At Tracys Landing, the earliest identified tobacco barn in
Anne Arundel County, and one of the earliest recorded
examples of its type in Tidewater Maryland.
(Maryland Historic Trust)

Since Maryland was not part of the Confederacy, it
was not covered by President Lincoln's 1863 Eman-
cipation Proclamation, which freed slaves only in the
states rebelling against the Union. In 1864, Maryland
adopted its own ban on slavery, in the context of a
new state constitution, which put it ahead of other
states where the practice was not banned until
passage of the 13th Amendment to the U.S. Constitution in 1865. But almost half (49.1 percent) of
Maryland's Black population was already free by the
beginning of the Civil War, including most of the large
Black population of Baltimore.

In 1815, Methodists and Quakers had formed the Protection Society of Maryland, to serve the growing number of free Blacks, many freed by their owners after the Revolution in response to Methodist and Quaker persuasion. Methodists, since the 18th century, had opposed slavery on religious grounds. However the church was not united on the issue and before the Civil War had split into two regional groups, one in favor and one against.

A PLACE CALLED FRIENDSHIP

In ante-bellum Southern Maryland, the tension over slavery was vividly evident in the tiny hamlet of Friendship, at the southern tip of Anne Arundel County, where tobacco barns dotted the gently rolling hills. The community, less than two square miles, included the cemeteries of its three Methodist churches, a parsonage, post office, two hotels and a few small businesses along Solomon's Island Road. This zigzagging route joined Annapolis, about 20 miles to the north, with tiny Solomon's Island, some 35 miles to the south. (In the 19th century the island was still using its original spelling, Solomon's, dating from its ownership by Isaac Solomon from 1865 to 1875. That spelling continued until the U.S. Board on Geographic Names, established in 1890, urged abandonment of apostrophes as part of the stan-dardization of geographic names, such as Solomon's Island, across the country.)

The original Calvert Circuit Methodist Episcopal
parsonage at Friendship, Maryland.
(Author's photo)

The fact that tiny Friendship had two Methodist
churches built by Whites within sight of each
other was the result of a dispute over slavery in
1862. A Black church, Carter's African Methodist
Episcopal Church, had been firmly planted long
before the war near the crossroads that formed the
center of the tiny hamlet.

Various historic records indicate the little enclave
at one time was known as Hell Corner, based on the

perceived wickedness of some of the people found there by Methodist preachers who passed through. One such preacher, while praying under two oak trees, was pelted with eggs and stones, until the owner of the property threatened to kill the attackers if they didn't stop the assault.

Whatever demons had once given rise to the name in this southern Anne Arundel community, by 1877 they seemed to have been driven out by the three churches adorning the landscape of the hamlet now known as Friendship.

In the late 1700s, zealous missionary activity by the Methodists in southern Anne Arundel and Calvert counties had weakened the hold of the Society of Friends, the Quakers, as they were known, which had been the area's dominant religious group since the mid-1600s. By 1877, the Quakers were long gone from the area. Again, a major reason was slavery, which Quaker teachings opposed, but which many tobacco farmers believed essential to their operations. A few freed their slaves, but most withdrew from the Society, and many joined the Methodists.

One of the largest land owners at Friendship was 55-year-old Sarah Plummer, a widow whose family on the side of her late husband Joseph were originally Quakers, dating back to the mid-1600s in the Maryland colony.

By 1877, with slavery a remnant of the past, labor-intensive tobacco cultivation on farms such as Mrs. Plummer's was predominantly the role of tenant farmers and sharecroppers, many of them former slaves. Sharecroppers owned neither the land nor the crops they cultivated but were paid for their labor with a portion of what they produced. Tenant farmers also did not own the land, but they often owned their own equipment and animals, and paid rent—typically about one-third the value of the crop—for the land and a house.

Both sharecroppers and tenants worked Mrs. Plummer's large farm. One of the tenant families was a young couple, the Norfolks. Henry, born in Sunderland, in Calvert County, was 25. His wife, 22-year-old Sarah (called Sallie by the family), was born nearby in Anne Arundel County. The couple had been married in 1872. They had three young daughters, Bertha, 4, Ida, 2, and a baby, just six weeks old, and as yet unnamed. They lived in Mrs. Plummer's two-story frame house, next to an orchard, adjoining a dense woods. The woods was skirted by a long clearing leading to a tobacco bed and cabbage patch.

THE DAY EVERYTHING CHANGED

Saturday, May 26, 1877 started out a typical spring workday on the Plummer property, or so it seemed. Afternoon temperatures were expected to reach a comfortable 71, after early morning lows in the 50s. About 8 o'clock in the morning, Sallie Norfolk left the house to collect salad greens for the midday meal from the cabbage patch next to her husband's tobacco bed. Wearing a bonnet and with a shawl wrapped around her shoulders in the cool morning air, she walked briskly to the garden near a thickly wooded area, about three quarters of a mile from the two-story, wood-frame house.

Around noon, when Henry Norfolk came back to the house for dinner, Mrs. Plummer's cook told him his wife had not yet returned. He asked two neighbors, the Stallings, to search for her.

Arriving at the tobacco bed, the Stallings found the young mother crumpled on the ground in a pool of blood. Her skull was crushed and one side of her face horribly mutilated. Her body was cold and stiff, and her blood clotted, indicating she had been dead several hours. Nearby lay the basket she had filled with greens. Now wilted, they provided additional evidence that the crime had been committed at an early hour.

About 60 yards from the body lay a hickory club an inch and a quarter in diameter and three to four feet long. One end was stained with blood, with what appeared to be strands of Sallie's dark blonde hair clinging to it. There were no signs of a struggle or any other marks of violence on her body or clothing.

News of the shocking discovery spread quickly. Neighbors started gathering at the Plummer property, horrified by what they heard and saw. Some whispered seamy rumors. Others passed along dark observations or chilling speculation.

The local coroner convened a jury of inquest that same afternoon, in accordance with Maryland law. Several witnesses were called before the session was adjourned for the night. The next day being Sunday, there would be early morning church services, including what would surely be a most heart-wrenching funeral.

3

LAYING TO REST

*It's so much darker when a light goes out than it
would have been if it had never shown.*

—John Steinbeck

Friendship M.E. Church was just large enough to
accommodate comfortably the regular congregants
from surrounding farms in this rural postal stop. But
this morning, the white-frame chapel was strained to
the rafters with mourners, most of them neighbors,
wishing to bid prayerful farewell to the murdered
Sallie Norfolk and comfort her grieving family. Sitting
with heads bowed in the first row of the chapel were
her father, farmer Uriah Johnson of West River,
about nine miles north of Friendship, and Alice
Johnson, her stepmother, whom he'd married after
the death of his first wife. The daughter whose body
now lay in the coffin a few feet away was the second
of five children born to Uriah and his first wife,
Ann Ward Johnson. Sallie was their first daughter.
Sitting beside Alice were Sallie's siblings, James, 24;
Elizabeth, 21; Samuel, 18; and Ella,16. It was agreed
that Sallie's children, still too young to understand
what was happening, had best remain at home.

What was strange in the moments before the
service began was the absence of Sallie's husband,

Henry. Hitching a horse-drawn wagon behind the church, one of the mourners noticed a man lingering under a cedar tree in the cemetery. It was Henry, standing alone, a figure almost six feet tall, and very round in build, weighing about 180 pounds. He had a dark complexion, a thick, ox-like neck, and flat, dark hair that grazed the broad eyebrows above his usually expressionless eyes.

The widower seemed to be staring toward the front of the church, but he made no movement in that direction. He would later be described in the numerous press accounts of the murder as a man with rough, coarse, and cold features, who bore himself "with the utmost stolidity." Some added observations such as "exceptionally calm," "unemotional," and even "indifferent" in the midst of what had to be the worst tragedy of his young life, and certainly the worst ever visited upon the quiet hamlet of Friendship.

Knowing the services were about to begin, the latecomer strode directly up to Henry. It would be very inappropriate, the neighbor told him solemnly, if he did not enter the chapel for the funeral of his wife. Henry neither responded nor moved. The mourner shook his head slightly in a gesture of perplexed futility, and left Henry in the church yard.

A COMMUNITY IN MOURNING

The congregation stood as the service began. Soulfully, they lifted their voices to the chords of a favorite hymn, many unable to contain their tears by the fourth verse:

> *In death's dark vale I fear no ill, with thee,*
>
> *dear Lord, beside me; thy rod and staff my*
>
> *comfort still, thy cross before to guide me.*
>
> —"The King of Love My Shepherd Is"

The Reverend Sinclair Neal delivered the eulogy. On a wooden catafalque to his left, the casket rested in front of the altar. There was a wreath of purple and blue pansies on its lid, which was never raised. It would have been too grisly a viewing, and to no one's benefit. The young woman's face had been smashed beyond recognition, her head seemingly reshaped into a ghastly geometric by the blows that had assailed it.

Everyone in the chapel knew how Sallie would have appeared, had she been standing with them before the savage act that had taken her life. She was known by all the faithful in the rural Methodist community. About 5 feet 6 inches, and "of fine stature and appearance," as *The Baltimore Sun* described her, "with a quiet and gentle disposition," the young mother of three was "highly esteemed by all her acquaintances." Of "prepossessing appearance" would be the descriptive most frequently used by newspapers across the country that followed the murder. It meant simply that the victim was an attractive woman.

These images of Sallie Norfolk were entangled this morning with the gruesome details revealed by the testimony of the first witnesses at the inquest opened the previous evening. Blood-curdling descriptions of the murder victim's fatal wounds now swarmed like locusts in the heads of mourners. One after another, witnesses had placed their hands on the Bible and sworn to details that were adding up to the most cold-blooded, grueling murder in local history. The thought of what someone had done to this young woman was gut wrenching. Thus the peace meant to descend upon a funeral congregation when realizing that the deceased is finally at rest, finally free of all earthly burdens, finally going home to glory—just wasn't there.

There was no sense of serenity or closure soothing these bowed heads. Competing instead against the visible outpouring of sadness was an equally obvious sense of outrage brewing across the pews. The Rev. Neal could feel it as he peered into the somber faces of the congregation. Some wiped away tears; others sang out while looking heavenward, as though this might dispel the images bombarding their brains. Others stared past him with jaws clamped tightly shut, as if something far more dangerous than the words of a hymn might escape from open lips.

Finally, the Rev. Neal stepped up to the pulpit. Speaking softly, he memorialized the short life of Sallie Norfolk, her good deeds, her kindness to neighbors and her love for the beautiful children she'd brought into this world—one just a few weeks earlier. Then, obviously aware of the volatile emotions swirling among what the newspapers described as a "highly excited" congregation, the clergyman's words took on a very different tone. Scanning the rows of mourners, he very pointedly urged them "to observe calmness and discretion in pursuit of the murderer."

Everyone knew exactly what he meant. Some among the rows of bowed heads were mumbling even now. The blunt language the good reverend did not use was *Don't leave here a lynch mob.*

4

THE INQUEST

Here, death rejoices in teaching the living.

—Inscription common in autopsy venues

Lynching, the word the Rev. Neal never mentioned but was obviously on his mind—and most likely the minds of others—was not uncommon in 19th century Maryland, or elsewhere in the country. It was a very real possibility for anyone even suspected, much less convicted, of committing an assault on a white female. While this was especially true if the suspect were Black, there had been lynchings of White men in Maryland, and would continue to be.

Nineteen years later, Joe Cocking, for example, would be lynched in nearby Charles County for murdering his wife and sister-in-law. Convinced of his guilt, local farmers found a delay in his trial date simply intolerable. Justice delayed, they seethed, was nothing short of justice denied.

A few days after Sallie's funeral, a front page report in the *Pittsburgh Post-Gazette*—fortunately not a local publication—included information that was not only fabricated but also potentially both prejudicial and incendiary. The newspaper reported that Sallie's clothes were torn, and that there was evidence of a "desperate struggle having taken place between the victim and her fiendish murderer." Neither was true, and Maryland newspapers had not reported these claims.

Suggestion of a woman's struggle, especially with her clothes being torn, would conjure up an attempted sexual assault. In a 19th century racially mixed society, such suspicions had often led to the lynching of a Black man without benefit of trial. And on the Plummer property there was a Black man whom Sallie's husband was already accusing.

During the investigation, Henry urged Sheriff Isaac Nutwell to arrest Joe Davis, who had been working in a field about 150 yards from the clearing where Sallie was killed. Davis was an illiterate 27-year-old father of two who worked as a farmhand on the property.

On the morning of the murder, he was working with another Black field hand, Daniel Thomas. Thomas testified that neither man had heard any cries, except that of Mrs. Stallings when she and her husband, sent by Henry to look for Sallie, had discovered her body, bloody and mutilated.

The sheriff refused, as there were no grounds for suspecting Davis. Sallie had been in the middle of a large clearing, surrounded by a thick bed of dry leaves. It was evident that she could have heard someone approaching her from any direction. Had anyone other than her husband approached her with a club, he reasoned, she would have cried out and attracted the attention of other nearby workers.

The sheriff's reaction didn't deter Henry. He tried to get his brother-in-law, John Armiger, to testify that Davis had a motive: He'd allegedly had a dispute with Henry over some piece of farm equipment. But Armiger refused.

When the inquest resumed on Monday, the evidence was all circumstantial, but the testimony spun out a damning picture in full detail. Henry Norfolk testified that he had been repairing a fence on Saturday, returning home about noon for lunch. When he asked the cook where his wife was, she answered that Sallie had not returned from her early morning foray to collect salad greens from the cabbage patch beside the tobacco bed. He seemed to be alarmed at her long absence and asked two neighbors, James Stallings and his wife, to go up to the meadow road that led to the tobacco bed and look for her, while he skirted the woods.

Within minutes, the Stallings found Sallie at the tobacco bed, lying face down, with her head resting on her arm. When Mrs. Stallings looked closer, she screamed at the sight of Sallie's smashed and bloodied head. They also noted the nearby basket of wilted greens and the bloodied club on the ground. The bushes several feet around were also spattered with blood.

Their hearts racing, they hurried back to Henry and breathlessly reported the horror they'd found. To their puzzlement, he was reluctant to go to the scene himself. When they finally convinced him to accompany them to the tobacco bed, he maintained an odd distance from the spectacle of his murdered wife with her head battered "to a shapeless mass." According to the Stallings, he betrayed not the least emotion.

Questioned at the inquest later in the day, Henry could give a satisfactory account for only about an hour of his time after leaving home around 7 a.m. until his return at noon. He said he had been cutting poles to mend a fence, which took about 45 minutes. He also admitted that he had cut the poles with the same axe now in Sheriff Nutwell's possession. Gaps in the poles he'd cut matched exactly gaps in the club with which Sallie had been murdered. All of these gaps corresponded to flaws in the blade of Henry's axe. It would be acknowledged later, however, that the axe was a woodpile tool that had been available to everyone on the farm, and since the club was dry hickory, it might have been cut as much as a month earlier. There was no way of knowing.

Henry further testified that he had no cause to kill his wife, that they never quarreled and that there was no jealousy between them.

Then the jury heard a peculiar story reported by James Stallings about a conversation he'd had with Henry the day before the murder. While the two men were working at the tobacco bed where the body was found, Henry allegedly had asked Stallings if he and his wife would take care of the Norfolks' six-week-old baby if Sallie should die. Then he asked another peculiar question: "We are here alone; if I should kill you, do you think anyone would ever find out that I did it?" The jurors sat stone-faced.

THE EXPERT

Spots that appeared to be blood had been noticed on Henry's pants and shoes. The sheriff confiscated the clothing and sent the articles to an expert for analysis. That expert was an authority so well known in Maryland that newspapers simply referred to him as "Professor Aiken." From the 1830s to 1888, William E.A. Aiken, M.D. was professor of chemistry and pharmacy at the University of Maryland. A graduate of New York State's Rensselaer Institute, he was one of three Maryland deans without a medical doctorate. The "M.D." frequently appended to his name was based on an honorary degree from the Vermont Academy of Medicine.

William E. A. Aiken, M.D.
(U.MD. School of Medicine Archives)

Prof. Aiken had been called upon for decades to provide expert trial testimony on his chemical analysis of evidence ranging from the contents of a deceased victim's stomach to blood samples from a crime scene. But his extremely diverse interests extended far beyond forensics. In 1852, for example, while teaching at the Baltimore campus, he constructed the city's first steam-powered "horseless carriage." The dust-covered but still-working model, believed to be one of the first of its kind in the world, was discovered among the medicine bottles and specimens in the university's pharmaceutical laboratory more than three decades after the professor retired.

A steam car model built by Dr. Aiken
at the University of Maryland in 1882.

Other Aiken contributions to Baltimore's industry and commerce included his 1868 certification of the purity of the Baltimore Condensed Milk Company's product. A few years earlier he had certified the safety of a "less stimulating" coffee mixture intended to be better for people with delicate digestive systems, and he gave his scientific thumbs up to a patented liquor purifier. More recently, in the same week as the Norfolk murder, he was mentioned in a classified ad for his whole-hearted endorsement of a name-brand gas stove. Serving also as a city inspector of gas and illuminating oils, he reported to the mayor on the quality of the oil and illuminating gas supplied to the city.

There was no question that Prof. Aiken was a household name. But his testimony, although considered important to the case against Henry Norfolk, would be limited by the science behind it. His stain analysis simply could not provide the level of forensic evidence possible today, or even conclusively prove the husband's guilt.

Although tests had been developed early in the 1800s to distinguish blood from other sources of stains, it wasn't until the 20th century that blood groups were identified, followed by discovery of a method for determining blood types. And it wasn't until 1895 that the first methodical study of blood spatters, such as those suspected on Henry's pants and shoes, was published. The study, coincidentally, would be titled, "Concerning the Origin, Shape,

Direction, and the Distribution of the Bloodstains Following Head Wounds Caused by Blows," by Dr. Eduard Piotrowski, at Poland's University of Krakow.

Thus, Prof. Aiken's analysis could determine little more than whether the stains on Henry's clothes were blood. He was not able to determine whose blood it was. (The first recorded use of forensic science to prove guilt also reportedly involved a farmer and a murder. In a 1325 case in China, a farmer was murdered in his field by a sickle, a common harvesting tool. When investigators collected all the sickles and laid them out, only one attracted flies, singling it out as the murder weapon.)

Proof that the stains on Henry's clothes were blood spatter was particularly important in this case in light of the absence of an eye witness and Henry's steadfast insistence of his innocence. Another possible cause of spatter, Henry's frequent nosebleeds, was ruled out as he had already denied having such a bleed near the time of the murder.

All the while the jury was taking in the testimony, then retiring to consider their decision, Henry Norfolk was described as remaining calm, displaying no emotion, seemingly removed from the gravity of the proceedings.

THE JURY DECIDES

It took the jury of inquest only minutes to reach a verdict. In a somber tone, the foreman reported to Justice of the Peace Hall that the 12 men unanimously believed sufficient evidence had been presented to conclude that Henry Norfolk had murdered his wife. Norfolk showed no emotion. The sheriff took him into custody immediately and led him away.

Inquest finding. (Maryland State Archives)

The record does not reveal which, if any, witness may have introduced the issue of motive into the testimony. Judging from various newspaper reports, it may have been the court of public opinion, and not the inquest itself, that suggested the answer. As one paper reported, "it is darkly rumored in the neighborhood of the atrocious crime that there is a woman at the bottom of the tragedy."

The Maryland Horror.

EXCITEMENT AT ANNAPOLIS.

The Husband of Mrs. Norfolk Committed to Jail—A Woman Said to be at the Bottom of the Case—A Probable Plea of Insanity.

ANNAPOLIS, May 29.—The shocking murder of Mrs. Sarah Norfolk has caused a thrill of horror throughout this community. A realization of the enormity of the crime culminated this morning when

The Daily Gazette (Wilmington, DE, May 31, 1877)

Another paper went further, identifying the rumored love interest as "a female relative of his wife." Another rumor reported in the press was that Henry's mother had remarked about three months earlier that she thought her son was going crazy. A plea of insanity, the reporter speculated, might be forthcoming at trial.

The murder was on the front page of newspapers as far away as Vermont, where the *Rutland Daily Globe* reported, "Mrs. Henry Norfolk, a white woman, was beaten to death in the woods near her residence at Friendship, Maryland on Saturday. Her husband is suspected." (May 30, 1877.)

Henry Norfolk was still steadfastly insisting he was innocent. By morning, he had retained two prominent lawyers as defense counsel: James Revell and Samuel Thomas McCullough. Revell, until the previous year, had been Maryland state's attorney for Anne Arundel County, an elected post, for 19 years.

James Revell, lead defense counsel.
(Circuit Court of Anne Arundel County)

McCullough, a native of Annapolis and an 1860 graduate of St. John's College, had served as a lieutenant in a Maryland Regiment of the Confederate army during the Civil War. (His wife, Nellie, was the daughter of Jedediah Hotchkiss, General Stonewall Jackson's map maker.) He was also the elected counsel to the Anne Arundel board of county commissioners. He never used his first name, going instead by "S. Thomas McCullough."

S. Thomas McCullough with his wife, Nellie, and a child.
(UVA, Small Special Collections)

5

THE ANNAPOLIS JAIL

It is said that no one truly knows a nation until one has been inside its jails.

—Nelson Mandela

Henry was taken immediately to the Annapolis jail to await convening of the Grand Jury in October, five months away. From the outset, he was reported to be "taking the situation very coolly," conversing freely about the murder, denying that he was guilty and asserting that he had no cause to kill his wife. He repeated that they had never quarreled and there was no jealousy between them.

Almost two weeks later, on June 6, Mrs. Plummer reportedly made a startling discovery. She was removing some rubbish from the dwelling when she found, carefully hidden away among some trash, a pair of work gloves that belonged to Norfolk. They were saturated with what appeared to be blood. She turned them over to Sheriff Nutwell.

In July, *The Baltimore Sun* reported that after more than a month in jail, Henry Norfolk had "during the whole period preserved the same imperturbable demeanor that characterized him at first."

"He talks cheerfully on all subjects, sleeps well and disposes of his meals with methodical regularity."

Several out-of-town newspapers (e.g., *The York [PA] Daily*, and Wilmington, Delaware's *Daily Gazette*) inexplicably reported exactly where he was confined in the jail—"the northeast room on the second floor"—and that he was with "five other white prisoners." Because of the insecure condition of the jail, prisoners charged with any serious crime were generally manacled to the floor, but these newspapers reported that Henry was "unironed." The report was practically a roadmap for a mob set upon removing him. It would not have been the first or last time it happened at the Annapolis jail.

All of these reports could have spelled trouble for Henry. His emotionless response to his wife's murder had stirred reactions ranging from puzzlement to outrage among the local population, repeatedly described in the press as "highly excited." Another irritant in this case, as in other high-profile Maryland cases, was the months-long wait until the next session of the court. More than one accused prisoner had been dragged from a Maryland jail by a mob unwilling to tolerate delay. And in Anne Arundel County, the jail was notorious for its lack of security.

A RICKETY OLD BUILDING

A few years earlier, a prisoner being held in another murder case told the warden the Annapolis jail was "the most rickety concern he was ever in." He claimed that on any night of his incarceration he could easily have "knocked the old Deputy Sheriff down and walked out." He didn't, however, "because the Deputy had treated him with so much kindness," and besides, he believed he would be acquitted by the jury. He'd had a key to the irons on his legs since the morning he was placed in the cell, when the deputy, after shackling him, had thrown his keys on the bed and left the cell for a few minutes. The prisoner quickly found the key that unlocked his shackles and put it in his boot, enabling him to remove the irons at pleasure when the deputy was not around.

Two years earlier, on June 7, 1875, a mob had broken into the same jail without difficulty, seized a Black prisoner, John Simms, and carried him to a lynching tree with alarming efficiency.

THE SIMMS LYNCHING

Whether John Simms was guilty of the heinous act with which he was charged we will never know. There was never a trial. The mob that lynched him claimed that in the moments before his execution he had confessed to the rape of a White woman. But that could also have been their way of justifying their own unlawful behavior. Their actions, reported in detail, read like a "how to" for an attack on the Annapolis jail.

Referring to the "old rickety building denominated a jail" where Simms was confined, *The Baltimore Sun* had called it "a most insecure place for prisoners," adding that it was only due to the most extreme care that those incarcerated within its precincts were kept from escaping. The paper warned that the sheriff "had better place a good guard around the jail," as "the old barn invites an easy entrance."

Given the horrible nature of the crime, the chief justice had called an extra session of the court's June term to be held in two weeks, beginning on June 30, to try the defendant. This news brought public expressions of satisfaction, as well as requests that there be no delay in Simms' sentencing and execution after conviction. In the aftermath, however, there were also allegations that this seeming satisfaction was a ploy meant to throw authorities off guard while plans proceeded for his lynching.

Shortly after his arrest, Simms had narrowly escaped an attempt by a lynch mob at Odenton to grab him from law officers taking him to Annapolis, about 15 miles away. Maryland Governor James Black Groome happened to be aboard a Baltimore & Potomac Railroad train passing nearby when he was informed of the mob and its purpose. He ordered the train stopped so the lawmen and their prisoner could be taken safely to the jail. The mob's plan was thwarted, but only for the moment.

At about nine o'clock the following Sunday night, as reported by the *Sun*, a band of at least 150 men, disguised with masks or blackened faces, convened as planned near Odenton to execute a new plan. The larger portion of the lynchers were on horseback, armed with guns and pistols, while some 15 or 20 of the party, unable to obtain horses, secured handcars of the Baltimore & Potomac Railroad. The horsemen started from Odenton at 10:30, and the handcar party about 90 minutes later. The whole party reached Annapolis at 2 a.m. and went immediately to the jail, on the west side of the town.

Reaching their target, they surrounded it while attempting to secure entrance by subterfuge. One member of the party, leading another man whose hands seemed tied behind his back as if he were under arrest, approached the door of the jail and rang the bell. The jailer appeared at the window and asked who was there. Invoking the name of an Annapolis policeman, the imposter replied, "Cairnes, with a prisoner."

The jailer wasn't fooled. "You're not Cairnes," he replied, "and you have no prisoner." The party decided that since the jailer had discovered their ruse, they would admit that they had not brought a prisoner but had come for one. Using a racist term for Simms, one of the lynchers warned the jailer they would use force if necessary to get him.

Then, at a signal from their leader, the mob at the back of the jail broke down the rear door. It took all of about two minutes. After battering in the woodwork, the men "crawled through the openings made between the iron bars and fastenings, which they were unable to force." Holding the jailer at pistol point, they proceeded toward Simms' jail cell. The jailer "fought bravely and desperately," according to the *Sun*, refusing to give up the keys to Simms' cell, or to tell them which of the three Black men in the jail was Simms. But the lynchers knew from accounts they'd received that he was the only one chained to the floor, and that's how they found him.

They broke the iron fastenings and carried Simms out of the jail. The lynchers tried to gag him, but he resisted and bit one of them on the hand. He was taken by handcar about two miles on the rails toward Baltimore. The preselected point for the hanging was a large white oak tree on a farm where a private road crossed the railroad tracks. Simms, a noose around his neck, was placed on a horse while the other end of the rope was fastened to a limb of the tree. The horse was then led from under the doomed man, and in 10 minutes, he was dead, The party of masked and disguised men then dispersed in various directions, not one ever identified.

Public reaction was later described as largely supportive of the lynching, both as a deterrent to future such crimes, and because it spared the young, female victim the embarrassment of having to appear at a trial. Between 1861 and 1933, there would be 46 lynchings in Maryland, all but four of the victims being African American.

NO IMPROVEMENT

Two decades later, the insecure condition of the Annapolis jail had been brought so often to the attention of county authorities that the Anne Arundel County sheriff concluded it would be "useless" to refer to it again. The occasion was the 1899 escape of "John Doe," most likely an alias, who was charged with horse theft. Using a portion of an iron bedstead, Doe had picked the mortar from the brick wall facing the street to the northwest of the jail. He made a hole large enough to admit his more than 6-foot frame, and while breakfast was being served to other inmates, jumped easily to the ground about 6 feet below. He then scaled a 6-foot high fence and disappeared.

The warden, it was said, had been talking to the prisoner a few minutes before he was missed from his cell, where he had carefully placed a blanket to hide the hole. Doe evidently had worked on it during the night. The sheriff admitted that of all the prisoners in the jail, the 40-ish, "very polite" John Doe was "the last one he would suspect of attempting to escape." The headline on the newspaper report was simply, "A Weak Old Jail."

The Annapolis jail was not the only site of questionable confinement in Southern Maryland. For decades, Calvert County's jail in Prince Frederick had often been cited as one of the worst in the state. Local authorities openly claimed that its poor condition served as a deterrent to crime. But as in Annapolis, it also made the jail an easy target for lynch mobs, as proven nine years later when a Black prisoner was dragged from his cell and hanged.

In 1877, the grand jury making its periodic inspection of the Calvert jail reported a fire hazard from a stove pipe passing through the ceiling in immediate contact with wood. They also found that no light was admitted to the front section of the jail without opening a shutter, which left the room too cold to be inhabited except in moderate weather. Other than that, jurors reported the jail was clean.

6

THE SUMMER OF THEIR DISCONTENT

The Great Strikes of 1877

Throughout the summer months, newspaper reports consistently described Henry as "in good spirits," and "confidently expecting his acquittal." If he harbored any concerns about vigilante action prior to the court's fall term, he never voiced it. Instead, he calmly insisted on his innocence, and in that he did not waiver.

Beyond the walls of the jail, Maryland cities and towns were coping with other challenges, and Baltimore more than most. The explosion that erupted on the streets and in the rail yards of Maryland's major commercial hub was not a sudden blast from nowhere. It had been four years in the making. In midsummer, 1877, outrage, financial ruin, and furious indignation reached the ignition point. Like workers all over the country, Baltimore's trainmen went on strike.

Since the end of the Civil War, the railroad industry had been a money maker and the nation's largest nonagricultural employer. But then one of the industry's major investors, a banking firm, found itself over extended and declared bankruptcy.

An economic panic, the Panic of 1873, swept the country. One bank's collapse quickly led to others, with about 18,000 businesses failing in just two years, including about 100 of the country's 364 railroads. By 1876, resultant unemployment had hit an alarming 14 percent.

In Baltimore, the B&O Railroad responded to the crisis in July 1877 by announcing a 10 percent cut in the wages of all employees making more than $1 a day and slashing work weeks to two or three days. Locomotive firemen immediately walked off the job, leading to other walkouts not only in Baltimore but also in West Virginia, Pittsburgh, and beyond. Tensions mounted as rumors spread throughout the city that troops were being brought in to confront the strikers. It was true, and the strikers were ready for them, meeting them head on, armed with stones they hurled at the soldiers.

Troops of the 6th Regiment, Maryland National Guard, open fire on strikers. *Harper's Weekly*, Aug. 11, 1877.

Although government forces were outnumbered, they were better armed, and casualties started to mount. There were almost a dozen at first, including a newsboy, a student, and a baker, all shot and killed. By August 1, the short-lived strike in Baltimore had ended, while still spreading across other parts of the country. The B&O had refused to give in on the 10 percent wage cut, but workers were promised fuller employment. The railmen had little choice but to accept.

LOCAL OPTION LAW

In Southern Maryland, the summer of 1877 was not only hot, it was also dry. In mid-spring, the Calvert County Board of Commissioners had voted to opt into Maryland's local option law. That was the law that gave every county in the state the authority to ban the sale of alcohol—if it chose to do so. Calvert County had chosen to do so. The temperance movement, having long agitated for government action to curb public drunkenness, had now succeeded in at least banning the sale, if not the consumption, of alcohol.

The editor of the local weekly had no sympathy for the afflicted:

> *Last Tuesday, being the first day of May, the Local Option law became operative in this county, and now from the dry throats of the followers of Bacchus is heard the husky wail of lamentation. To those*

*who have been accustomed for so many years to get from the country stores their precious 'nips,' their 'pints' or their 'half pints,' the experience of the past week must have been particularly harrowing. No longer on a Saturday evening will be seen the smiling crowd at this or that store, but mournful and lengthened visages will meet the gaze. Like ghosts of their former selves, 'they will gather 'round the counter,' not to drink alas! but to discuss in sepulchral tones their cruel fate and gaze piteously upon the empty barrel which lingers there, how tantalizing to them—how suggestive of days when they were 'glorious, o'er all the ills of life victorious.' And then to return to their homes sober, without even a 'stirrup cup' [parting drink] to keep out the cold or allay the heat, how forlorn they will feel, and how we pity them. To come down to cold water will doubtless be hard lines for many of them, but to such a fate they will have to come or one still more **bitter**. We believe that in time they will all take kindly enough to water, and when at the end of the year they find themselves with better health, happier houses and money in their pockets, they will not regret the banishment of King Alcohol.*

Solomon's Island had just been sold for the second time since 1875 when Isaac Solomon walked away from the oyster canning enterprise that had converted the island from farmland to a major waterman's community. The first buyer, a Baltimore investment company, had announced plans to convert the tiny sand spit into a summer resort. But they bailed out after just two years, perhaps realizing the new law would hardly be conducive to summertime beach parties. The new owners, having announced similar plans for the strip of land at the mouth of the Patuxent, may not have realized what was happening. Under the local option law, Solomon's Island suddenly seemed a less desirable site for a rollicking summer resort for deep-pocket vacationers from Baltimore, Washington, D.C., and beyond. It would instead be a dry summer on the island and throughout Calvert County.

When the May term of the Circuit Court for Calvert County opened on May 10, Judge George Brent delivered an impressive charge to the grand jury, dwelling on the good result to be gained by the proper enforcement of the local option law. He intimated that no evasions of the law ought to be tolerated and was particularly severe toward the venders of bitters, a mixture of bad whisky and noxious drugs. Acting on this advice, the grand jury immediately indicted several of the county's liquor dealers. Their trials were scheduled forthwith.

But Solomon's was still a waterman's community, and watermen are known to seek any port in a storm. That summer, they found it at the wharf at the eastern tip of the island. The Weems Steamboat Company made call at Solomon's three times a week, and while the boats were loading and unloading cargo and passengers, the islanders were welcomed aboard to patronize the bar. Every steamboat boasted its own bar.

The steamboat wharf at Solomon's Island.
(Calvert Marine Museum, Solomons, Md.)

For Solomon's Islanders, it was like a mini-holiday three times a week—a holiday, that is, from the hated local option law. But as the saying goes, all good things must come to an end. For Calvert County, the summer holidays came to an early end when the county commissioners caught wind of the capers at the wharves and ordered the steamboat line to close its bars when visiting any port in the county. It was just September 1.

The *Calvert Journal* had another snarky editorial to mark the occasion:

> *This is indeed 'hard lines' for the 'boys' who have been reveling all Summer in steamboat whisky, and from Plum Point to Lyons Creek a wail of anguish is heard. In this dry and barren country the steamboats had got to be Oases to the suffering ones, and as grateful as the ships to the starving people of Ireland during the great famine, were they to the dusty pilgrims who waited on the wharf and shore for their arrival. But now alas! the steamboats are to them no longer things of joy, but horrid, old, basin-stained sepulchers in which lie buried all their fond anticipations of a good time during the peach season. Cut off in this way from their loved 'nips' by the cruel hand of the Agent of the Weems' Line, we see no resort for the boys but a stern determination, cost what it may, to put up with cold water.*

The local option law was invoked in other counties as well. Anne Arundel followed suit five years later, under the Act of 1882, Chap. 112. But the law was never considered a success.

Temperance groups charged that it had too many loopholes, while anti-prohibitionists complained it had too few. In the end, the experience soured the populace so much that decades later, when the 18th Amendment to the federal Constitution—the Prohibition Amendment—was ratified in 1919, Maryland was the only state in the Union that refused to enact local enforcement laws.

Fifty-five years earlier, Maryland had won the nickname the "Free State" when it adopted a constitution that abolished slavery within its borders. Now that moniker applied once again for another reason, and Marylanders reveled in it. Calvert County, having learned a tough lesson from the local option law, would work hard in the future to assure that the county board of commissioners always included at least one liquor store owner.

7

GRAND JURY

*A grand jury hears only one side
—the prosecutor's.*

It would be five long, hot, and typically humid months before Henry Norfolk would leave the Annapolis jail for his first appearance in court. The next session of the Anne Arundel County Circuit Court was scheduled to begin on the third Monday in October. The courthouse stood on the southwest of the capital's Church Circle. The large court room was on the first floor. Above it, on the second floor were the jury rooms. On September 2, Chief Judge Oliver Miller drew the names of the members of the grand jury as well as the petit jury pool that would serve during that session.

When he convened the court in October, Judge Miller commented that under Maryland law, it was the duty of the grand jury to visit the jail, to inquire into the way the prisoners were kept, as well as the condition of the jail, and to make a report. "The condition of the jail," he continued, "has been the subject of report from successive grand juries from time to time as a building unsafe and insecure and prisoners are unnecessarily crowded in rooms where they would be no more safe than in other parts."

Later in the month, the grand jury reported back to the court that they had visited the jail and "found it neat and cleanly," but as their predecessors had similarly observed, it was "insecure." The inmates, however, were "comfortably provided with food, bed furniture and other necessities."

Anne Arundel County Courthouse, early 1800s; https://www.circuitcourt.org/about-us/court-history.

After being in session 10 days, the grand jury reported that, in addition to visiting the jail and taking care of other business, it had investigated 67 cases, examined 132 witnesses, and dismissed 24 cases "which were of trivial character." Unlike a trial jury, a grand jury does not determine the guilt or innocence of a person suspected or accused of a crime. Instead, the panel meets in secret to hear only the evidence presented by a prosecutor, and then to determine whether it is sufficient to justify a formal charge against someone.

FOUR MURDER INDICTMENTS

The grand jury had decided in favor of murder indictments in four cases. The four men indicted were arraigned on October 19. Arraignment in Maryland is an accused person's first appearance in the courthouse. It's the time when the judge informs the prisoner of the crimes set forth in an indictment, outlines the maximum penalties associated with each charge and allows the person to enter a plea of "guilty," "not guilty," or "no contest."

Of the four men arraigned, the most infamous among them, and the one whose appearance had drawn the crowd, including news reporters, to the Circuit Court that morning, was Henry Norfolk. According to *The Baltimore Sun*, there was a noticeable buzzing, a "sensation among the spectators," as Henry walked to the dock, where they "eagerly watched" his every move:

> *He was carefully dressed for the occasion. He was entirely self-possessed, and bore remarkably well the scrutiny of the hundreds of eyes leveled at him. Stolidness seems a prominent part of his character, and is plainly shown in his countenance.*

Cover of Indictment
(Maryland State Archives)

Directed by the judge to read the indictment, Major Sprigg Harwood, Clerk of the Circuit Court, began in a clear tone, articulating every syllable of the jury's handwritten, damning charge that Henry Norfolk:

> *not having the fear of God before his eyes but being moved and seduced by the instigation of the devil, on the twenty sixth day of May in the year of Our Lord one thousand eight hundred and seventy seven, with force and arms...on and upon one Sallie Norfolk in the peace of God... thinking feloniously, wilfully and of his malice aforethought did make an assault;*

The indictment went on to describe the weapon as "a certain large stick of no value" with which, the jury charged, Henry had struck Sallie on the left side of her head, dealing her a mortal wound two inches long and an inch deep, of which she instantly died.

Harwood concluded the reading with the usual inquiry, "Are you guilty or not?" But the words were hardly out of the clerk's mouth when Henry "distinctly and energetically" replied, "Not guilty."

The other three men arraigned that morning were: Richard Lloyd, "colored," charged with the murder of his wife; Andrew Hammond, charged with the murder of Joshua Saffield; and William Edgar, charged with the murder of Mary Davis, "colored." All pleaded "not guilty." Of the four indicted, only Henry Norfolk and Richard Lloyd had been held in the Annapolis jail since May. Hammond and Edgar were charged with murders committed in September and October.

Richard Lloyd was an elderly Black man, described as quite lame. He was charged with the murder of his wife on the 13th of May, by shooting her with a gun. He was intoxicated at the time and claimed that the shooting was accidental.

Andrew Hammond was scheduled to be tried on October 23 for the murder of Joshua Saffield in what was described as a "rough and tumble fight," a drunken brawl at Odenton on September 2. There was evidence of a scuffle and fisticuffs between the two men, during which Hammond was accused of kicking Saffield to death.

William Edgar was charged with killing Mary Gibbs, "colored," on October 6 by shooting her through the heart. They were quarreling about some cattle, when the woman allegedly pointed a gun at Edgar. He claimed he fired while she was taking aim, and she fell to the ground dead.

These last three were tried and convicted by October 27. Henry's trial was certain to last longer, after the state's attorney announced that he would call 20 witnesses for the prosecution. He expected the trial would begin the following Monday, October 29.

A newspaper report described Henry as being "in good spirits," and confidently expecting acquittal. "But," the report ominously added, "there is more in his case than he imagines, and more than the public has yet known."

8

A DAY AT THE RACES

The Great Contest Between East and West

Some 40 miles from Annapolis, yet light years away in terms of the business of the day, horse racing history was being made at Maryland's Pimlico Race Course on October 24, 1877. Even Congress was interested. After declaring a day's adjournment, members of the U. S. Senate, as well as most of the House of Representatives, boarded a special train of the Western Maryland Railroad that ran on a spur from Arlington, Virginia, all the way to the grandstand. Since its opening in 1870, the race track, the second oldest in the country (after Saratoga in upstate New York), typically attracted an audience arriving in a parade of horse-drawn carriages. The race on this day, however, would become a page in horse-racing history, as "the race that Congress adjourned to see."

The event had been advertised as "The Great Contest Between the East and West." The big attraction was a handsome, compactly built, five-year-old bay with a long, shaggy mane named Ten Broeck. He was named after Richard Ten Broeck, a horse-racing pioneer, and the first American ever to race American-bred horses in Great Britain. In three years of racing, the stallion had captured all the important stakes in his native Kentucky, breaking every time record at distances from one to three miles. But he'd never raced in the East, despite at least one high-dollar invitation to compete at Saratoga.

Members clubhouse at Pimlico, oldest building in American racing, dating back to 1870.
(Library of Congress)

So epic was the Kentuckian's track record that when his owner, Frank Harper, finally brought him to Baltimore and announced that his horse would race, most of the potential competition backed away. But not the Lorillard brothers. George and Pierre Lorillard were scions of the oldest tobacco manufacturing company in the country. Both were also major players and frequent competitors on the thoroughbred horse racing circuit.

George owned an enormous colt that surpassed all contemporaries at 17 hands (68 inches) high with a girth of 76 inches. He was named Thomas Ochiltree after Colonel Thomas P. Ochiltree, another larger-than-life figure, who joined the Texas Rangers at age 14 and fought for the Confederacy during the Civil War. Col. Ochiltree's career over the next four decades included political appointments, a newspaper editorship and election to the United States Congress from Texas.

Pierre Lorillard entered his thoroughbred Parole in the race. During most of his early years, Parole was considered the best juvenile racing. Still, neither thoroughbred boasted a record as stunning as Ten Broeck's. In 1877 alone, the Kentucky wonder had won eight races in a row, three of them run solely against the clock, since no one would enter against him.

On this Wednesday, a record crowd filled the stands, expecting not just a race, as exciting as it might prove to be, but also chomping at the bit (pardon the pun) to see the greatest horse of his time in action. Several members of New York's American Jockey Club had arrived along with a large delegation headed by August Belmont, the financier, diplomat, and sportsman whose name adorns the oldest and longest of the three classic horse races that constitute the Triple Crown of American horse racing. There was also, as might be expected, a large contingent from Kentucky, staying at Barnum's City Hotel, where the Clarence M. Mitchell Jr. Courthouse stands today.

A front page story in *The Baltimore Sun* would report that "the grandstand bloomed with the beauty of the fair daughters of Baltimore" and the field in front was brilliant with "rich costumes and handsome women."

When the race began, Tom Ochiltree sprang forward on the dry track, setting the pace. But as large as he was, he could not sustain the lead against his faster Kentucky rival, and he fell off. Ten Broeck's supremacy, however, was short-lived, as Parole flew forward, passing both Ochiltree and then Ten Broeck, to finish the two-and-a-half mile race by a lead of four lengths. According to the *Sun*, Parole crossed the finish line amidst:

> *the wildest shouts and most extravagant demonstrations of delight. Before the jockeys could dismount, the quarter stretch was invaded by hundreds of men who leaped the pickets and frantically embraced the winner. One man kissed the noble creature.*
>
> *The victorious jockey was borne in triumph on the shoulders of men and placed on the fence, where his cap was quickly filled up with money. Cheer after cheer went up from the immense assemblage and the few who became winners by the generally unexpected result were the gainers by immense odds. The losers, on the other*

*hand, were almost ruined. Someone said
that the Kentuckians would have to walk
home for want of funds to pay their fare,
so completely did the result clean them
out. The only consolation left them was
that it took two to do it. Many said it
was Parole that took the money, but Tom
Ochiltree who won it for him.*

An illustration of the historic finish is immortalized on the
Pimlico clubhouse, symbolizing the legendary races it has
hosted over more than a century and a half.

Parole went on racing until he was 12 years old,
America's leading money winner and the best gelding
of his era. He died on January 1, 1903, at age 30.
Ten Broeck continued racing in Kentucky, where his
1878 match race against the great California mare
Mollie McCarty was immortalized in the Kentucky
folk song "Molly and Tenbrooks." His headstone was
the first ever erected for a thoroughbred in the state
of Kentucky. After retiring to stud, Tom Ochiltree
died in 1897, eventually joining his famous rivals in
horse racing's Hall of Fame.

9

THE TRIAL

A court is only as sound as its jury, and a jury
is only as sound as the people who make it up.

—Atticus Finch in *To Kill a Mockingbird*

The trial of Henry Norfolk for the murder of his wife was called as scheduled before Judge Oliver Miller on Monday morning, October 29. But when the names of witnesses were called, it was discovered that a large number for both the State and the defense were absent. The Court ordered attachments to be issued for the missing witnesses and continued the case until the next morning.

Judge Oliver Miller
(Circuit Court of Anne Arundel County)

DAY ONE

When the court reconvened on Tuesday morning, a large crowd filled the courtroom. The state's attorney, Henry Aisquith, was assisted by James H. Hodges. Henry Norfolk was represented by Revell and McCullough. The first order of business was selection of the jury, which the court concluded with dispatch. The names of the 12 men selected were published in *The Baltimore Sun* the next day, along with a summary of the testimony heard.

The State's first witness, Dr. George Pembroke, testified as to the cause of Sallie Norfolk's death, and that he had found human hair in congealed blood on the club apparently used for the murder. Another witness testified that the indentations on the club corresponded with those that would be made by the jagged blade of an axe owned by the defendant. The spectators remained silent as they listened to these opening salvos.

Richard Drury, postmaster of the village of Friendship, was next on the witness stand. He testified that before the murder, Norfolk had asked him if a murderer touched a corpse, would blood flow from it. This strange question related to a centuries-old superstition that if a murderer touched the body of his victim, blood would indeed flow from it, an indication that the victim was identifying its slayer. It was a type of trial by ordeal called "cruentation," from the Latin *cruentatio*, staining with blood.

Cruentation involved bringing the accused before the corpse of the murder victim and requiring him to put his hands on it. Sometimes the mere presence of the murderer would cause the corpse to bleed (perhaps explaining Henry's distancing himself from his wife's corpse from the moment it was discovered, even refusing to enter the church for her funeral). Cruentation was admissible evidence at an alleged murderer's trial in the United States until at least the mid-1800s.

At the inquest, Drury also had noticed red spots on Norfolk's hat and asked the defendant to let him look at it. Norfolk had balked, replying, "Do you think I killed my wife?" The witness testified that he thought the spots were indeed blood. At this point, the Court took a recess.

When the Court reconvened for an evening session, there was damning testimony about Norfolk cursing and threatening to strike his wife, and saying, "Why did she have so many infernal girl babies?" Those words caused an audible stir, amid a shifting of bodies in the courtroom. Some members of the jury appeared to wince or recoil ever so slightly. Then there was testimony that the first time Norfolk saw Sallie's dead body in the presence of witnesses, he had said, "Sallie is dead—let's take her home." These witnesses agreed that before the body was moved, Norfolk had seemed more interested in the arrival of people at the crime scene than in the pitiful sight of his murdered wife. The court adjourned for the night.

DAY TWO

There were again many spectators in the courtroom when the trial resumed on Wednesday. First on the stand was Prof. Aiken, the chemist, to whom the state had sent the clothes Norfolk had been wearing the day of the murder. Standing 6 feet tall, with a flowing white beard, the expert testified with certainty and precision. He told the court that he had by chemical and microscopic tests examined Norfolk's pants, shirt, and boots, and that the spots on the shirt and boots were positively mammal blood. He said those on the pants were not so positively blood, but indicated blood. There was so much foreign matter mixed into these stains that their analysis could not be as clear as the others.

After a recess, Prof. Aiken was cross-examined by the defense. He acknowledged there was no way of telling how long blood spots had been on any surface.

The State put several other witnesses on the stand, including Joe Davis and Daniel Thomas, Black men who had been working in a bed near the scene of the murder. They testified that they had heard no cries on the morning the deed was committed. But they did hear Mrs. Stallings crying when the body was found and had immediately come over to the murder scene.

Two other witnesses testified that Norfolk had sworn at the coroner's inquest that he left his house about 7 o'clock on the morning of the murder to fix a neighbor's fence, and that he got back to the tobacco bed where James and his brother Alexander Stallings were working at half-past eight or nine. The Stallings claimed he had not appeared at that field until 10:45.

Several witnesses also testified that Norfolk had wanted Joe Davis arrested, based on no more than his assertion that Davis had a grudge against him because he would not sell Davis a turkey on trust. But Davis testified that he never wanted to buy a turkey from Norfolk. The defendant's brother, Benjamin Norfolk, also testified that Henry had asked him to swear that he had overheard Joe Davis' wife accuse her husband of murdering Sallie and say he had better leave. Benjamin Norfolk would not do it, despite his brother's pleading that unless he did, Henry would be suspected and would suffer.

Mrs. Plummer, who owned the farm and shared her house with the Norfolk family, testified that she had seen Henry on the morning of the murder, with an axe and something she thought to be a gun in his hand, climbing over the fence in the direction of the site where his wife was found. So convinced was she that it was a gun, she said she had expected to hear its report.

And then Mrs. Plummer said something that seemed to spike the interest of both the jury and the roomful of spectators. She testified that she had seen Miss Ella Johnson, Sallie's younger sister (16 years old at the time of the murder), go into the barn and stable with Henry several times and stay in there together five minutes.

Late in the afternoon, the State closed its case. The defense opened immediately with the testimony of Henry's mother. She testified that there had always been good feelings between her son and his wife. She observed that people react differently to grief, and that Henry would look sad when in mourning but did not cry. She said she had seen blood on his shirt and pants on the evening before the murder and had asked him about it. He'd said his nose had been bleeding.

(But this was contradicted by Norfolk's alleged statement to another witness that he had not had a nosebleed.)

She then identified Henry's clothes as the same garments she saw him wearing at the time of the murder.

Eliza Griffith, a Black woman, testified that she was midwife to Sallie, and that Henry had stuck by his wife during her confinement.

Testimony asserting Henry's good character followed, but on cross-examination none of the witnesses could prove that they'd ever heard his reputation discussed. The testimony of several witnesses portrayed the defendant as an ignorant, superstitious, brutal man. Not long before the murder, one witness testified, Henry had said to his wife, "Sallie, I had my fortune told in Baltimore, and an old woman told me I would have three girls;

the youngest would live 12 months; I would live the longest, and would marry a girl of 17. And there is something else which if I told you would grieve you to death."

Henry's father, James Norfolk, contradicted some other statements of the State's witnesses, but none was very important.

The court adjourned until the next morning, after the defense said it would finish in an hour, perhaps calling the defendant himself.

DAY THREE

When the trial resumed on Thursday morning, the defense called an F.L. Griffith to the stand. He had been directed to measure the work done in the tobacco bed before and after Henry got there, according to what James Stallings showed him. Contrary to James Stallings' testimony, Griffith concluded that Norfolk must have gotten to the bed when he said he did, between 9 and 10 o'clock, whereas Stallings swore it was about 10:45.

Then it was Henry Norfolk's turn. Knowing full well the risks, his attorneys put him on the witness stand in his own defense. At this point in the trial, it seemed his only chance.

The room was as quiet as a morgue as Henry testified that he left the house about 8 o'clock on the morning of the murder. He said he went to fix a neighbor's fence, and took with him an axe and a gun. It took him 20 minutes to get there. After working on the fence for from half to three-quarters of an hour, he returned to the tobacco bed, where James Stallings was. Henry admitted that he had asked Stallings about whether the dead body of a murdered person would bleed if the murderer touched it. But he explained that he'd been talking or thinking about a murder case tried in Annapolis just a week earlier, with no apparent relevance to the case at hand.

Part of the time Henry was testifying, his voice was so low it was impossible to hear him 10 yards away. The last of his testimony was confined mostly to contradicting the statements of others or explaining his own suspicious words. He said that his nose had bled the day before the murder, and he supposed that was how blood got on his clothes. He said he'd forgotten about it when he told one of the witnesses that his nose had not bled.

CLOSING ARGUMENTS

After a brief recess, the court called for closing arguments. Leading off, James Hodges, of counsel for the State, summarized the testimony of the prosecution's witnesses over the three days of trial, arguing for conclusions the jury should draw from each. Among the most telling was his argument that when the defendant was seen going over the fence with an axe and something else in his hand, it was not a gun but a club.

McCullough rose next, arguing for the defense. He claimed that if Norfolk were hanged, it would be on the testimony of witnesses who had been contradicted by other witnesses. Norfolk, he reasoned, could not have killed his wife because he was in the field at work with James Drury between 9 and 10 o'clock. He cited the case of a man in England who was next heir to a child he was overheard to be correcting, when the child cried out, "Don't kill me." She disappeared the next morning. He was arrested and required by the court to produce the child. Not being able to do so, he got a child to impersonate the missing one. After the fraud was detected, he was tried, condemned, and executed. Five or six years later, the missing child, then 16 years old, returned. She had run away to another county, where she'd been cared for.

At the close of McCullough's story, the court ordered a recess until half-past four o'clock. The jurors would need every minute of it to ready themselves for defense attorney Revell's two-and-a-half hour closing argument. The seasoned trial lawyer was well aware that the argument he put before the court in that time could mean the difference between life and death for his client. For the past three days he had poured everything he had into cross-examination of the state's 20 or so witnesses, challenging their recollection of details whether meaningless or pertinent to the outcome of the case, questioning their objectivity and, where possible, their credibility. He had studied the reactions of the jury to every nuanced response to State's Attorney Aisquith from the neighbors working in nearby tobacco beds when Sallie was murdered. They have no proof, he kept telling himself. It's all circumstantial. And they don't like this man because he's odd.

Revell had seen this kind of bias before. In fact, he thought he'd seen almost everything in his 19 years as state's attorney for Anne Arundel County, the elected post he'd held until just the year before, that now was held by Aisquith. An exceptionally likable fellow with a solid family history (his father, for one example, was postmaster of Annapolis), he was also a lawyer's lawyer. His experience as a prosecutor enabled him to see the weaknesses in the government's case and target them as if shooting down waterfowl on the Bay.

But this case would take more than that. Somebody had brutally clubbed a young woman to death, and in the five months since that May morning no other suspect had been identified. No one other than the husband whose unfortunate appearance was repeatedly described in the newspapers as "brutish." If you look the part, Revell sneered to himself, you must be guilty! Revell would have to do more, and he knew what it was. But first, he had put Henry Norfolk on the witness stand in his own defense, a risky move in most criminal cases and one never taken without serious consideration of the potential consequences.

Henry had been "cleaned up" for the occasion, which had been preceded before the trial by an unusual photo shoot with the Annapolis newspaper's hired photographer. Henry's hair, previously described as hanging over his dark brows, was now slicked back in a gentlemanly fashion. Instead of his rough farming garb, he was decked out in a white shirt with starched collar and a serious necktie, punctuating a conservative suit. Instead of the cocky, almost boisterous attitude he'd displayed all these months while proclaiming his innocence, he'd been coached to speak softly and appear modest, humble, sincere—nothing he reportedly was accustomed to, the result being a voice so low, he could barely be heard.

But that was over and done. Whether it had any effect on the jury, Revell was unable to tell. Their faces were like blank slates. It was now up to the lawyer to take his last, best shot. And Revell was armed and loaded.

For two and a half hours, he tore apart the testimony of every damaging witness. But he knew he'd have to go further. There had to be another possibility. Another suspect. Another man in that field on May 26 who could have committed this heinous crime. Revell didn't have to prove someone else's guilt. He just had to infuse enough possibility into the scenario that a reasonable juror would have difficulty sending a man to the gallows unless it were ruled out. Ruling another suspect out was not his responsibility. Nor could the prosecutor do it at this point. The facts had been presented. If they had not foreclosed the possibility of another killer, it was too late. James Revell cocked his weapon and set his sight on the target: Alexander Stallings.

The 19-year-old had been working in the neighboring tobacco bed with his older brother, James, on the morning of the murder. The teenager had sworn that he'd never left his plow the whole morning in the field next to Henry's. But the testimony of another State's witness indicated he was lying. He'd allegedly been seen coming from the place where Sallie had been murdered. He was lucky, Revell said, speaking slowly, that his clothes, unlike Henry's, had not been subjected to chemical analysis. After pausing for that thought to sink in, the lawyer clarified that he was not saying he "suspected" Alexander, adding "suspicions are nothing."

He knew full well, however, that in this case, suspicions might determine the outcome. If that was not enough to cause doubt in at least one juror's mind, he reminded the panel that Alexander's testimony had been impeached—and not by the defense, but by another of the State's own witnesses. Shaking his head at the seemingly inevitable conclusion, Revell declared, "If he was proved false in one, he was false in all."

Returning to the defense table, Revell glanced toward his client, expecting to see some reaction. But Henry was expressionless, staring straight ahead at nothing.

Attorney Aisquith rose next to close the case for the State. He traced Henry's movements on the morning of the murder, which he argued had to have been committed at half-past nine. No stranger had committed this horrid deed, he declared, it was someone in whom the victim had confidence. The folded bonnet, the unspilled cabbage plants in the basket, and the absence of cries were all mute witnesses, he said, while the gapped axe and club spoke volumes. On top of that, all day before the killing, the subject of Henry's conversation had been murder. All the evidence, Aisquith concluded in summary, pointed to Henry Norfolk as the murderer of his wife.

At 10 o'clock that evening the case was given to the jury. After receiving instructions from the judge, the 12 men retired, "amid the most profound silence in the courtroom," according to a reporter, although the benches were filled with spectators. At half-past eleven, the jury was still out, and would remain so for the night.

TRAGEDY ON SOLOMON'S ISLAND

The Friday when Henry Norfolk's guilt or innocence was argued before the Annapolis jury was a dramatic day elsewhere in Southern Maryland as well. Solomon's Island was drenched in rain all day. Gale-force winds added to the day's drama, as waves pounded its shores. Dr. Virgil Lawrence, the island's resident physician, was riding home on horseback from house calls elsewhere in Calvert County when he encountered water up to five feet deep across the shell road connecting the island with the mainland. That fragile causeway had been built by Isaac Solomon more than a decade earlier to facilitate passage between the mainland and the island, originally separated by some 500 feet of open water.

The driving rain, coupled with the deep water and unstable surface, apparently caused the horse to shy. The saddle-girth must have broken at the same time, throwing Dr. Lawrence into 18 feet of water on one side of the causeway. The horse returned home without its saddle or rider. Neighbors of the doctor immediately set out to find him. Using lanterns to light the way around the rain-drenched north shore of the island, they searched in vain for any sign of the doctor. It was too dark, and the wind and rain reduced visibility to no more than a few yards.

The next morning the search resumed before 6 a.m. In the early morning light, the searchers first spotted the doctor's hat floating in the tide, and then his body, washed up on the shore, with the saddle nearby, gentle waves now lapping against both.

Just 45 years old, Dr. Lawrence was an 1857 graduate of the University of Maryland School of Medicine. He'd written his dissertation on typhoid fever, an intestinal infection caused by contaminated food or water. With the Civil War less than a decade away, his subject couldn't have been more timely:

two-thirds of deaths during the war would be from disease, with typhoid fever the deadliest.

Dr. Lawrence had practiced in Anne Arundel County before moving to Solomon's, where his mourners described him as a "citizen greatly esteemed." He left a widow, but no children.

10

THE VERDICT

Each man must reach his own verdict,
by weighing all the relevant evidence.
—Leonard Peikoff, philosopher

On November 3, Sheriff Nutwell escorted the four inmates who had been tried for murder back before Judge Miller. Three were appearing for sentencing, while the fourth, Henry Norfolk, was still awaiting the verdict of the jury.

Chief Judge Miller began by calling for Andrew Hammond to be brought to the bar. The prosecution having failed to prove any malice, the jury had returned a verdict of manslaughter in the killing of Joshua Saffield. Judge Miller told the prisoner that he had taken several factors into consideration in deciding Hammond's sentence, including the fact that no deadly weapon had been used, the killing occurred during a fist fight, and it was not premeditated. Furthermore, Hammond had not started the fight, and was trying to get out of it. For these reasons, Judge Miller would sentence him to only six months in jail. Hammond was ultimately pardoned by Gov. Carroll, one of 70 executive pardons issued over the next two years.

William Edgar, who killed Mary Davis (consistently identified as "colored," in accordance with the custom of the time), with a shot gun, was next brought to the dock, where a prisoner stands during trial. He had also been convicted of manslaughter, rather than murder. The judge told him that the court must inflict such punishment on him as would "prevent others from this reckless use of firearms against human life." He said he took into consideration the jury's recommendation of mercy, but still believed Edgar should serve time. He sentenced him to one year in the Maryland penitentiary.

Richard Lloyd, convicted of manslaughter in the killing of his wife, was sentenced next. Judge Miller told him he did not think he intended to kill his wife, but he ought not to have been drunk. He added that Lloyd had not shown the love that he owed his wife, but in consideration of his good character and the prisoner's behavior when he became sober, he would sentence him to just nine months in the penitentiary.

Judge Miller had barely finished sentencing Lloyd when there was a stir outside the courtroom. The jury in the case of Henry Norfolk was returning from their deliberations.

The prisoner stiffened as the bailiff led him to the box. He fidgeted nervously as the jurors entered the courtroom and walked single file to their seats in the jury box. His eyes, usually so dull and devoid of any emotion, now seemed to roll about, while his body made slight jerking movements. The clerk asked the jury if they had agreed upon a verdict.

They had. There was not a sound in the courtroom as the foreman replied for the panel: "Guilty of murder in the first degree."

Henry's face flushed deep red. He looked at Judge Miller as if expecting the judge to impose the death penalty on him in the next breath. Instead, James Revell demanded that the jury be polled. Every juror stood up as his name was called. He then looked upon the prisoner and said aloud, "guilty of murder in the first degree." Some of the men were very decisive in their answers, while others gave their verdicts with evident emotion, in very slow and moderate tones.

Taking the prisoner from the courtroom, Sheriff Nutwell delivered him back to the jail. Henry's demeanor was very different from the night before when, anticipating acquittal, he'd been good-humored, laughing, and talking. He'd even claimed he did not want a compromise verdict of second degree murder, saying he expected to go home, and invited the warden to exhibit him around town before he did. This morning, however, apparently stunned by the verdict, he seemed a broken man, crying as he was taken to the jail, the first tears he'd shed since being imprisoned. Referring to his wife, he repeatedly moaned, according to press reports, "She gave me too many girl babies!"

Back in his cell, he asked the sheriff not to lock him in the floor irons, which the lawman was about to do for the first time. But the sheriff told him it was for his own good. Henry sobbed that he never would be hung, as he would grieve himself to death in two weeks. There was no statement from his counsel about whether they planned to appeal.

Two days later, Henry was described as abstaining from any nourishment whatever, except for a light breakfast on the morning of November 5. He was said to be "completely unnerved," with "paroxysms of grief and despondency" becoming more apparent as he realized the likelihood that he would not escape the gallows.

Chained to the floor, with everything save his bed removed from the cell to preclude any attempt at suicide—it had been reported that he had threatened to kill himself if he were convicted—he was told by a deputy warden on Sunday morning that the only thing left for him was to look to God through the medium of a spiritual adviser. Henry turned from the man and dissolved in a flood of tears. In desperation, he sent for his father and asked that his children be brought to him. He had not seen them since his imprisonment almost seven months earlier. He also indicated he would be sending for a minister.

11

THE DEATH SENTENCE

Capital punishment is the most
premeditated of murders.

—Albert Camus

Sheriff Nutwell arrived at the Annapolis jail shortly after lunch on November 12 to return his prisoner to the court for sentencing by Judge Miller. It had been just over a week since the jury had found Henry guilty of first degree murder and he was led sobbing from the courthouse. The following Wednesday, he'd been visited by the Rev. Dr. John Dashiell, pastor of the First Methodist Church, who reported that Henry was recovering his spirits and was no longer in such a "melancholy mood" as when he'd first heard the verdict against him.

The next day, another Methodist minister, the Rev. Mr. Lemon, reported after visiting Henry that he had shown no sign of making a confession, and therefore no evidence of repentance for the deed of which he'd been convicted. His hope, rather, was that the governor would intervene and commute his sentence to imprisonment in the penitentiary. When Warden White had attempted to reason with him, he'd replied that White did not know what the governor would do. He appeared, according to the visitor, "almost as cheerful as he was before his conviction," and "did not seem to realize in the least that he must soon die."

Henry maintained his composure as he stood before Judge Miller at 1:15 p.m. the following Monday. When the judge asked him if he had anything to say as to why sentence should not be pronounced, he answered: "I am convicted an innocent man; that is all I have to say."

The judge then said that he had been found guilty by one of the most impartial and intelligent juries that could have been selected and there was no doubt of his guilt. The judge added that he would not harass or harrow up the feelings of the convicted man by a recital of the horrible circumstances attending the commission of the crime. He advised him instead to look only to God for mercy, as he could expect none from any earthly tribunal. Finally, Judge Miller passed the usual death sentence, during which he seemed more visibly affected than the prisoner. Onlookers noted that Henry seemed at least nervous, while "his usually red face became blanched to an ashen hue."

A motion for a new trial was made by Henry's counsel but was denied by the Court.

A DEATH WARRANT
FOR A CONDEMNED MAN

Three days after his sentencing by Judge Miller, Henry was visited in his jail cell at 10 a.m. by a delegation that included Sheriff Nutwell, defense counsel McCullough, Warden White, a constable, and two representatives of the Baltimore press. His counsel explained the purpose of the visit: "Henry, the sheriff has come to perform a very unpleasant duty—to read to you your death warrant. He does not wish to do it, but it is his duty."

Henry replied, "Yes, sir."

Sheriff Nutwell then reiterated, "I am very sorry to have to do it."

Henry had been reclining on his bed when the delegation arrived, but by now had raised himself up to a sitting position. His leg irons did not allow him to move around his cell, which a reporter described as a "model of cleanliness." His lawyer sat on a chair beside him, while the others stood around his bed. His face flushed, Henry kept his eyes on the floor and never raised them while Sheriff Nutwell read, in a tremulous voice, the terrible mandate of the law:

> *The State of Maryland: To the sheriff of Anne Arundel county greeting. Whereas Henry Norfolk was convicted in the Circuit Court for Anne Arundel county, at October term, in the year 1877, of murder in the first degree, and whereas the said court sentenced him to be hung by the neck until he be dead, now, therefore, these are to will and require, as also to charge and command you, that, at or*

before the hour of two o'clock P.M., on Friday, the 21st day of December next, you take the said Henry Norfolk from your prison, and him safely convey to the gallows in the county aforesaid, the place of execution of malefactors, and then and there the said Henry Norfolk hang by the neck until he be dead. For all which this shall be your sufficient power and authority. Given under my hand and the great seal of the State of Maryland, at the city of Annapolis, on this 14th day of November, in the year of our Lord 1877, and of the independence of the United States the 101st.

By the Governor, John Lee Carroll

The silence that followed the reading of the warrant was broken by Warden White telling Mr. McCullough that Henry wanted to see his father. None of his friends or relatives had been to visit him since his conviction, although he had repeatedly asked for them. After some conversation regarding how a message could be gotten to the senior Norfolk, defense counsel asked to be alone with his client, and the others withdrew.

Shortly afterward, the Revs. Dashiell and Lemon returned to the Annapolis jail for a second visit with Henry. This time they found him in incessant tears.

THE GOVERNOR

Defense counsel were planning an immediate request to the governor to commute Henry's death sentence to life imprisonment in the penitentiary. Aside from the legal arguments around the circumstantial nature of the evidence presented at trial and the contradictions of witness testimony, there was much sentiment in the community that Henry was not only an obviously ignorant man, but likely mentally ill. Although he had not claimed an insanity defense, there had been speculation, including comments in the press, that he would likely do so.

On the other side, there was strong sentiment against any reprieve due to Henry's betrayal of "the most sacred relation" to his victim, which had left innocent babes without a protector. There was also the fact that he had displayed sufficient cunning to commit the "hellish deed" and then charge it upon a Black man. Finally, although the evidence was circumstantial, the chain was so complete that not the slightest link connecting him with the crime was missing.

On November 19, attorneys Revell and McCullough had their audience with Governor Carroll, the 37th governor of Maryland, and the father of nine children. He could not be moved. The governor stated that it was impossible for him to interfere with the execution of the law. He explained that responsibility for the conviction of Henry Norfolk rested entirely with the court and jury, and his duty was only to order that the sentence they had passed be carried out. The power of pardon and commutation, he argued, was given to the executive to protect a prisoner in cases where there appeared after conviction a reasonable doubt of his guilt. Unless evidence that established such doubt were shown to him, he could not interfere.

A CHANGE OF COURSE

The following morning, Henry's legal counsel visited their client to tell him the results of their meeting the day before with the governor. When told of the governor's response to their request for commutation of the death sentence, Henry was reported to have taken it "stoically." They told him there was no earthly hope, and he had better turn his attention to spiritual matters in preparation for the fate that awaited him. Henry listened quietly, and then asked Revell and McCullough to return in the afternoon.

He also met that morning with his father. It was James Norfolk's first visit since his son's conviction. He stayed for an hour, praying with him. James had always been a religious man, who insisted his children attend church and Sunday school.

Henry's four-year-old daughter was not permitted to visit him, as it was not known what impression it might make upon her. His younger daughter was sick with the measles.

Henry's legal counsel returned in the afternoon as he'd requested. When they left, they seemed extremely strained by the meeting, but refused to disclose anything they'd discussed. The lawyers' heads were bowed, and their faces unreadable as they hurried past a couple of reporters trying to ask questions about the meeting.

12

CONVERSION, CONFESSION, BLAME, AND FORGIVENESS

*Conversion without a clean heart
can only be a matter for sorrow.*

—Mahatma Gandhi

For weeks after his conviction and sentencing, Henry's demeanor was often described as "surly." He showed no interest in the fate awaiting him and refused the advice that he start to consider his spiritual condition. In early December, his counsel asked Governor Carroll to grant a respite of 30 days from the scheduled execution date of December 21. When he refused, Henry received the decision without any outward reaction.

Finally, the combined efforts of the two Methodist clergymen who had visited him, reinforced by a delegation of the Young Men's Christian Association of Annapolis, seemed to bear fruit. One week after he'd heard the final word from counsel that there was no chance of a reprieve from the governor, Henry received a delegation of church members in his cell. After emotional prayers and invocations, he bowed his head and quietly professed his conversion, adding that he was ready to die. The next morning, he issued a statement that he had been converted and was ready to go whenever the Lord called. He added that he expected to meet his wife and children in Heaven. He would not give up his "experience of forgiveness for ten thousand worlds."

Henry also handed a letter to a correspondent of *The Baltimore Sun*, which published it in full:

> *Annapolis Jail, Dec. 1, 1877—To the Public: I take this method of returning my sincere and heartfelt thanks to the officers and all who are connected with this institution for their untiring efforts to make me comfortable while I have been under their charge. Words are almost inadequate to express my feelings towards the warden (Allen White) who has ever been willing to come at my call or gratify my slightest wish or desire. In fact, he has been by my side day and night since my conviction, rendering not only to the wants of the body, but has aided those who have my spiritual welfare under consideration; and I thank God that through their instrumentality I have gained remission for all my sins, and I am perfectly reconciled to my fate, believing in a crucified Saviour who suffered and died for us all. I recognize fully that my*

days are few, and I will have to appear before the judgment seat of Christ, there to render an account for the deeds done in the body. I desire also to express my sincere gratitude to my counsel, who have been unremitting in their efforts in my behalf, and not slacking in any respect even since my conviction. I could not have been defended more ably nor more faithfully. I return also my thanks to the members of the Young Men's Christian Association, and all others who have kindly visited me since I have been in prison.

R. HENRY NORFOLK.

The only thing missing, several observers noted, was any hint of repentance or remorse, and it certainly was not a confession.

HISTORY ON THE NEWSSTANDS

By now newspapers across the country were following the story of the horrific murder in rural Southern Maryland. On December 6, a new daily would join the ranks, this time in the nation's capital. The first issue of *The Washington Post* was four pages, with seven columns to a page, filled with the latest news of interest to a local population of about 130,000, including daily congressional coverage, and sharp, aggressive editorials. Without telephones or automobiles, reporters covered assignments on foot or horse-drawn hacks, and sometimes even on bicycles. Stories from Annapolis, Baltimore, and beyond came in by telegraph.

The Evening Star, publishing from 1852 to 1982, and known at various times as the *Washington Star-News* and the *Washington Star*, was for most of its existence the newspaper of record in the nation's capital. The *Star* somewhat dourly reported the appearance of its new competitor with a reference to the newcomer's alleged advocacy of "schemes for depleting the treasury of the United States," which, it reported, *The Post* disclaimed.

WE OFFER $200 REWARD!

The POST Is Desirous of Securing a Copy of Its First Issue, Dec. 6th, 1877—Also a Photograph of its First Home at 914 or 916 Pennsylvania Ave.—It Hereby Offers $100 Each for the Desired Paper and Photo to the First Reader Presenting Either One or Both in Good Condition at This Office—Read Full Details and Look Through Your Mementos of an Earlier Generation—You May Find $200!

Should Have Saved a Copy:
On Oct. 28, 1928, *The Washington Post* offered a reward for a copy of its first edition on Dec. 6, 1877. The winner was the Washington News Exchange, which owned thousands of copies and files of old newspapers and periodicals.

When *The Post's* Annapolis correspondent reported the latest update on the Norfolk murder on December 7, 1877, it was disappointing. According to the reporter, Henry Norfolk had been expected "in all probability" to make a public confession the day before, but for the absence of one of his attorneys, who was ill. It was said, according to the reporter, that Henry was about to make "a clean breast of the whole matter," as well as reveal the motive for the murder. But he wanted his lawyers present, as well as the press. During the past evening, he'd been visited again by a delegation from the Young Men's Christian Association, who conducted religious services in which the prisoner took an active part, singing and praying.

The second biggest story out of Annapolis that day was the question of whether cows should continue to run at large within the city limits. Petition after petition, both pro and con, had been submitted to the city council, which had finally decided to put the issue to a popular vote the following January.

THE TRUTH AT LAST

Five days later, December 11, 1877, Henry Norfolk finally made his stomach-churning confession, describing in gruesome detail how he had murdered his 22-year-old wife, the mother of their three young children, on the morning of May 26:

> *I left my house ten minutes before 8 in the morning, my wife leaving about the same time. She went to the tobacco bed to get cabbage sprouts and took a different direction from myself. I went from the house right down where Stallings was plowing, crossed the bridge and went up the meadow toward the tobacco bed. We*

both got to the tobacco bed about the same time. Some words might have passed between us but nothing unpleasant. My wife did not expect me there. I cut the cabbage plants. I gave her the basket after I cut the plants. She started for home ahead of me. When I gave her the basket she said she did not think there were enough greens. When she reached the beech-tree under which she was killed I raised the club to kill her, but my heart failed me, and I could not do it. When we got out of the woods I told her to come back and I would cut her more sprouts. After the plants were cut she started for home again. I was behind her, and just as she got to the tree I struck her on the left side of the head, holding the club in both hands. Her bonnet was on then, and flew off at the first blow. The basket fell off her arm and did not overturn, as she fell with her face to the ground. She tried to get up and I saw her full face, and then I struck her four or five blows more. She never uttered a word or cry after the first blow.

Henry explained that he'd gone next to his neighbor's property, where he'd cut one pole, and put it in its place on the fence. From there, he went to the tobacco bed.

I got there between nine and half-past nine o'clock. Stallings was about the middle of the bed when I got there, and I commenced to work right alongside of him, and finished the breadth before we went to dinner, between half-past eleven and twelve. On my way to dinner I stopped at Mrs. Stallings to get a yeast cake, which my wife had asked me to get before I left home that morning. I had been thinking of killing my wife three or four months before I did so, and made up my mind on the Wednesday previous to the Saturday of the killing. On Wednesday I cut the club at the wood pile with my hatchet; it was a new hatchet, but was gaped; the axe shown in court had nothing to do with cutting the club. After I had cut the club I put it in the cornhouse, where it remained until Saturday morning, when I took it out as I started for the tobacco bed, and when I passed Stallings, who was plowing in the field, I had it down my pants leg, and took it out after I crossed the bridge.

Beyond the expected revulsion, reaction to Henry's confession was met with disappointment because he had failed to reveal his motive in committing the atrocious deed. The next morning, he did so, in a supplemental statement to *The Baltimore Sun*, in which he admitted that he had first thought about killing Sallie at Christmas, when he thought of using poison, but had abandoned the idea:

> *The counsel left to me to give or not my motive. It was to marry Ella, my wife's sister. She knew nothing of my intentions to kill my wife, nor did anyone. I never had any criminal intimacy with Ella, and only thought from her general actions and words that she would marry me if I was freed from my wife. This drew my affections from my wife...*
>
> *When I first tried to kill my wife my arm was so paralyzed that I could not raise up the stick. When I made the second attempt I struck the first blow on the left side of the head, the second on the front of the face—that was when the blood spattered upon the tree; the third blow I struck I hit my wife in the stomach. The rest I gave on the head. There were some seven or eight licks altogether. As soon as the deed was committed I repented of it, and would have given anything to have recalled it.*

Henry told the newspaper that his affections for Ella were waning when his wife became ill around the first of May and asked him to bring her 16-year-old sister to the house. He recalled that he did not want to go, because he was afraid of the consequences it might have for him. In retrospect, he thought that had he never gone for her at that time, he would never have committed the murder. His wife, he stated, never suspected anything. He added that he no longer cared for Ella.

Asked by a reporter if he did not think he would be found out after the murder, he smilingly replied, "No; if I had thought so I would not have done it. I was awaiting my opportunity for several days and thought that Saturday morning was my best chance." In answer to another question, he said that he expected to meet his wife in heaven. To the reporters present, Henry did not seem to realize the horror of the execution that would come first.

JUST AS GUILTY

On the same day, Henry sent Ella a rambling, accusatory, and at times incoherent letter, which he had written several days earlier:

December 5, 1877

MISS ELLA JOHNSON: I thought I would write you a few lines to know, and ask you to inform me, of your feelings, if you have any, of this sad fate of mine. You know full well that you are the whole cause of my trouble, and it is all on your account that so soon I have to suffer death. If you have any feelings they must be touched, and you be very careful hereafter how you trifle with married men, particularly your sister's husband, and also for swearing falsely against me at the trial, as you did. But I freely forgive you all the harm that you have done me, and I hope the Lord may forgive you, and that He may have mercy on your soul, and if you don't feel that He has forgiven you, you had better pray that He may forgive you, for you know that you have acted very wrong toward me and your dear sister, who is now dead, and in the sight of God and man you are just as guilty morally as I am, and my advice to you is to ask God to forgive you, and the only way is to ask Him in prayer, and if He don't forgive you, may Christ have mercy on your soul, for it was all on your account, and pretty actions and ways to me that I committed the deed, and you know well that it was all your fault, and your conscience must be condemned, if you have any, and I hope these few words will be a warning to you hereafter. I write these few lines to you as a friend, and I hope you will take them as such. As God has forgiven me all my sins, I hope in my prayers He will forgive all that you have done to me and your dear sister Sallie, who, I hope, is now in heaven. And I also forgive all the rest of

*the family who swore falsely against me,
and may God in His richest mercy bless
them—these are my dying words. So
formerly friends, now I must leave you, all
my earthly hopes are over, but in heaven I
hope to greet you there to meet to part no
more. When these few days are wasted,
and my dying scenes are over, I shall rise
to fall no more.*

R. HENRY NORFOLK

The defamatory public letter was published in newspapers across the country. Within a week, Ella Johnson, now 17 years old, and her father, Uriah, denounced the prisoner severely in their own letters to *The Baltimore Sun*, indignantly refuting Henry's charge that Ella was the cause of the murder, and that she had sworn falsely on the witness stand. The editors dismissed Norfolk's scandalous public letter, writing that both Johnsons seemed to attach more importance to it than it was worth.

Neither Henry's confession nor his letter to Ella mentioned the complaint he'd voiced after his conviction about his wife bearing too many "girl babies." By this time, the youngest of the three, just six weeks old at the time of Sallie's murder, had died, having never even been named.

Henry, meanwhile, was reported to be exhibiting freakish behavior. He was said to have declared that the hangman's rope would never go around his neck, and that he had something to take his life at any time. He was suspected of having a knife, but when he was moved to another cell and stripped, nothing was found. Then he claimed he had a razor blade and had thrown it into the fire, but there was no trace of it in the ashes.

His disposition since being transferred to another cell was described as very bad, and he declared that he would see no one nor eat anything until returned to his former cell. Subsequently, the handle of a small pewter spoon was found in his bedding. After taking proper precautions, Sheriff Wells allowed him to return to his original place of confinement.

13

THE GALLOWS

Nothing so concentrates the mind
as the sight of the gallows.

—Samuel Johnson

As his day of execution drew nigh, Henry was visited daily at the jail by ministers of the Gospel and members of the YMCA. One newspaper called them "professional soul-savers." It was also reported that occasionally "a number of kind-hearted Christian ladies called upon him and held religious exercises in his cell." It was said that Henry joined in these services with ardor, his "peculiar bass voice" carrying beyond the others, giving a sepulchral effect to their sacred songs. At the urging of counsel, the sheriff allowed Henry's shackles to be removed for these religious services.

The erection of the scaffold began on Wednesday morning, in plain view of the window in Henry's cell. The sight completely unnerved him. The hammering added to his terror, as he moaned and wept on his bed. By three o'clock Thursday afternoon, a platform had been erected 11 feet above the ground, reached by 15 steps. It had a cross-beam about 7 feet above it, and a trap-hole in the center 3 feet 2 inches square. Henry, weighing between 170 and 180 pounds, would fall about three-and-a-half feet. The rope was five-eighths of an inch in diameter, and between 30 to 40 feet long, sufficient to allow his body to be lowered after death. The drop of the scaffold was worked by a new invention, which the sheriff would trigger upon descending to the last step of the gallows.

Shortly after sunset, the deputy warden brought Henry his last supper, but he declined to touch it, his head bowed, and his hands clasped as if in prayer. At 8:30 p.m. his spiritual advisers arrived to find him kneeling by his bed. They included members of the Young Men's Christian Association and four clergymen. He told them he had experienced a religious transformation. They later revealed that Henry seemed to realize his approaching doom, and was frequently moved to tears, at times sobbing aloud.

They stayed with him until 10:30 p.m., leaving him in prayer by himself. At midnight, he arose from these devotions and asked the night watchman for ham and bread, which he ate greedily before retiring at 12:45 a.m.

THE FINAL HOURS

Henry's last day dawned dark and dank. It was Friday, the day with a reputation as the favorite day on which to carry out the death penalty. The statistics bore that out. In 1877, 47 murderers were hanged across the U.S. on Fridays, as opposed to 36 on all other days of the week combined. He had asked that he be hanged early in the morning to escape the gaze of a large crowd. It was a futile request. Daylight revealed that the entire fencing around the north, east and south sides of the jail yard was covered with people of every race and color. Soon the rooftops were crowded. One eventually caved in from the unaccustomed weight.

Henry arose at 4 a.m. and indulged in religious devotions until 8:15. Shortly after, a committee of the Young Men's Christian Association, accompanied by two clergymen, entered his cell and had prayers for nearly three hours, during which Henry frequently buried his face in his handkerchief and sobbed convulsively.

Before the clergymen withdrew to allow the prisoner to meet privately with his brother-in-law, John Armiger, Henry reportedly "had burst forth into a flood of ecstasy and spoke beautifully," as one clergyman expressed it, "beyond his intelligence," thanking those who had defended him and those who had given him spiritual counsel. He said that he felt Jesus near, and made the comment, most likely referring to his own baby girl, that he could see "a child which died when a few months old, beckoning for him to come." He was sure he would meet Jesus there as his Savior. Although he expressed dread at the ordeal of death, he said he did not fear it because he had peace within. He would walk up the scaffold like a man, he vowed, and die with Jesus near him.

John Armiger informed Henry that he would take his body to Friendship for burial, although not in the same lot with his wife and child. Henry seemed pleased and expressed his gratitude as he bade Armiger farewell. A few minutes later, he met for the last time with his counsel, Revell and McCullough.

By this time, the crowd surrounding the jail yard had swelled to thousands (some newspapers reporting as many as 5,000 people). Sheriff John B. Wells, who had just recently succeeded Isaac Nutwell in that office, had decided to make the execution "private," having about 280 tickets printed for the occasion. He was reported to be overrun with requests from people desiring to witness the execution, but declined to issue more tickets. While only a limited number, including some "well-dressed ladies," were admitted into the jail yard, where the scaffold was erected, the hanging would be anything but private. The gallows was visible to thousands, both Black and White, who would witness it from the streets beyond the gates.

Shortly after 11 a.m., Sheriff Wells and Warden White entered Henry's cell, where he stood waiting, plainly dressed in a well-worn, dark suit, a white shirt with rolling collar and black tie, and wearing a pair of gaitor-boots (a short version of which had become popular for urban wear in the late 1800s).

Carrying a rope to bind the prisoner's arms, the sheriff simply told Henry that his time had come. Calmly asking that his arms not be tied as yet, Henry explained that he had something to say on the scaffold and could say it better with his arms free. The sheriff agreed, and the execution procession exited the cell, with Sheriff Wells on one side of Henry and Warden White on the other.

As they emerged, Henry found his counsel, Revell and McCullough, standing in wait. Both men appeared overcome with grief as Henry affectionately embraced them. Barely getting the words out, they wished him a good deliverance.

FIFTEEN STEPS

As he had promised his church supporters, Henry did ascend the 15 steps of the scaffold with firmness, accompanied by the sheriff, the warden, two clergymen and a representative of the press. Upon reaching the platform, he was told by Sheriff Wells that he could say whatever he desired. According to one report, "while his features were not particularly bad, he displayed a repulsive countenance, as he stood erect and glanced hastily around the crowd," addressing the assembly in a loud, clear voice:

> *My Friends—I thank you all for your kindness to me. Take warning from my fate. I killed my wife, and now must suffer death! O, take warning, young men, for I must be hung for what I did! But I thank God that he sent me good friends, who have shown me the way to Jesus, and I have found remission for all my sins, and*

*am going home to glory. Yes, I expect to
go to Heaven, and will meet you no more
on this earth, but hope to meet you on the
other shore.*

Henry then thanked his counsel, who, he said, had
stood by him "like two brothers." With that, each of
the clergymen offered a solemn prayer for the soul of
the condemned man, after which Henry whispered, "I
see nothing dark; all is bright before me."

All except Sheriff Wells then descended the steps of
the scaffold. Taking the cord from his inside pocket,
the sheriff proceeded to pinion Henry's arms and then
legs, while the prisoner repeatedly bid "good-bye" to
his friends, asking them to meet him in heaven.

After placing a white cap over Henry's face, Wells
drew the noose around his neck. It appeared, however,
that the sheriff was making the rope too tight, as
Henry turned toward him and said something, after
which Wells adjusted it. The sheriff then turned
and descended the steps, pausing half-way down
to manipulate the mechanism that controlled the
scaffold. With that, the trap-door opened beneath the
doomed man's feet.

For a moment he hung motionless, but soon the
horror of what was happening came into view. Henry
began convulsing, whirling around, drawing his legs
up, and making desperate but futile efforts to free his
hands and feet. Minutes later his body was lowered,
and a team of doctors pronounced him dead.

Henry's corpse was placed in a walnut coffin and removed in a wagon to a burial ground at Friendship where his father had purchased a lot. Contrary to reports that the people of Friendship did not want him, that was where he would be buried. But not beside Sallie. And there would be no marker on his grave.

REACTION

The entire execution was conducted, it was agreed, with "perfect perfection," with Sheriff Wells commended for his "calm and collected manner."

In his final hours, Henry had refused to see any strangers, turning away Baltimore and Washington reporters who tried in vain to interview him. About a week earlier, he'd sat down with a reporter and photographer from a local Annapolis weekly, even allowing the photographer, F.M. Zuller, to take his photograph.

While Fuller was setting up for the shoot, Henry gave the reporter a brief synopsis of his life, mentioning that he turned 26 the same month he killed his wife, whom he described as a most amiable woman, as so declared by all who knew her. He repeated that nothing ever happened during their married life to mar the happiness of either, and that to fulfill her every desire was his pleasure. At this point, the reporter abruptly interrupted his account of Henry's interview to express his puzzlement at that statement:

Yet this man...fondled his innocent and trusting wife for five long months with foul and cold-blooded murder in his heart. When the fatal infatuation took possession of that heart, which seemed too relentless and unfeeling ever to have experienced the sensation of love, he was converted from a man into a brute, and committed the blackest crime that a demon could possibly execute. The annals of our county or State do not show a more revolting murder, and it has sent him igno-miniously from the world with scarcely a sympathetic pulsation of the human heart for his miserable end.

On the same page, the editor of this newspaper, the *Maryland Republican and State Capital Advertiser*, which claimed the largest circulation in Annapolis, wrote a stinging commentary on the Norfolk case. The editor's outrage was palpable. It read in part:

Now, we have on hand the case of Norfolk—we beg pardon, we should call his name with more reverence—Mr. R. Henry Norfolk. He has earned complete absolution and remission by a signally bloody murder; but who is prepared to say that this Christian study would be in the good condition he is if he had not beat his poor wife's brains out? Moses and

*the prophets had he; he lived in a land
full of churches; he had heard preaching
and joined in prayers, but they were of
no avail. One stroke of a good club did
more than all the provision made by the
churches would have done had he lived
to the age of ninety years. He has now
emigrated, for to him death is but a step
to change worlds when he leaves this
to reach the shore, where the butchered
wife stands eager to welcome him and all
his applauding relatives who have gone
before will give three angelic cheers and
a "tiger" over his glorious arrival. And he
will wait for those whom he now leaves
behind, having first kindly instructed
them to "follow him." His forgiveness we
all have, too, and a general invitation to
that mansion which he fancies is to be
given completely to his charge.*

The Associated Press, whose coverage of the hanging was carried by newspapers across the country, also reflected the incredibility of statements Henry had made in his final weeks, topping its report with the headline, "The Hanging of a Model Husband."

Another newspaper in Oakland, in western Maryland, was disgusted by the scene at the gallows, using the occasion to denounce public (but not private) executions in general:

Norfolk, the murderer of his wife, suffered death by hanging Friday, at Annapolis. He expressed confidence in the forgiveness of his sins, and in his immediate transfer to Heaven, but did not extend the usual invitation to the spectators to meet him in that better land. His omission to do so may have been on account of the low character of the crowd collected to witness the hanging. It consisted chiefly of negroes and boys, some of them of tender years. Whiskey added to the demoralizing influences of the scene; and one of the spectators, so far from receiving kindly the warning of the fate of Norfolk, took that occasion to beat in the head of a fellow-man with a brick. Public executions are the worst lessons which can be taught to a crowd.

In 1913, hangings were moved from public space to an area within the prison obscured from public view. A century later, Gov. Martin O'Malley signed a bill outlawing capital punishment, making Maryland the 18th state to abolish the death penalty.

There were no other commentaries on the Norfolk execution in any of the still preserved periodicals across the country. Even the photograph of him all cleaned up for F.M. Zuller's camera on the eve of his execution was cut from the newspaper before it was archived. It was as if the devil might still peer from the killer's eyes, piercing the soul of the unwary.

Henry's expressions of repentance, it seemed, were meant to perfectly reflect the requirements of a religious tenet, and no more. There was no outpouring of remorse to the children whose mother he had murdered, or to his own mother who would petition the court for custody of the little girls left orphaned. (Sarah Norfolk was issued guardianship papers for the children in Calvert County in 1888.) Nothing except, "I killed my wife and now must suffer death...I have found remission for all my sins, and am going home to glory." The path to glory, as the repulsed Annapolis newspaper editor put it in undisguised outrage, was guaranteed by "one stroke of a good club."

POSTSCRIPT

Beyond Henry Norfolk's immediate family, it is likely that no one felt worse about his ultimate fate than his defense attorneys. Revell and McCullough had believed his unwavering protestations of innocence. They had put him on the witness stand without knowing that he was about to lie after swearing an oath before God to tell the truth. Not until the eve of his public confession had he admitted his guilt to them.

His lead defense counsel, James Revell, having served the state of Maryland as one of its chief prosecutors for almost two decades before returning to private practice just months before this case, was probably better prepared for the truth. From his base in the state capital, he had seen every type of miscreant known to Maryland society and had heard, he thought, every hue of falsehood from the "little white lie" to the blackest distortions of reality. As disappointed as he likely was in the outcome of this major case, he moved on, practicing as defense counsel for some 15 years before rising to the bench as an associate judge of the circuit court of Anne Arundel County.

Thomas McCullough was a battle-tested veteran of the Civil War, having fought for the Confederacy as a member of Company D, Second Maryland Line, and surviving as a prisoner-of-war on Johnson's Island, Ohio, when General Lee surrendered. But his subsequent legal career—and perhaps his life—

might have ended within months of Henry Norfolk's execution had a bizarre scenario involving State's Attorney Henry Aisquith played out differently.

In early September, 1878, while en route by train from Annapolis to Baltimore, Aisquith made some highly offensive remarks to a companion about local judges and attorneys in general, but McCullough specifically. McCullough, who was then counsellor to the board of Anne Arundel County commissioners, was sitting nearby and overheard the remarks.

He stepped up and confronted Aisquith, denouncing him in the most emphatic terms. Aisquith responded by swinging at McCullough with a closed fist, which was parried by McCullough, who followed through with several blows, striking Aisquith in the face. McCullough then jumped on the seat and kicked Aisquith in the chest. Other passengers stepped in and separated the combatants. Asquith offered an apology for his remarks which McCullough refused to accept.

According to reports at the time, McCullough later sent Aisquith a grossly insulting letter, and Asquith, concluding that nothing but blood would atone for the disgrace, left Maryland to consult with a man in Pennsylvania well acquainted with the rules of dueling, which was banned in Maryland. The man consented to act as Aisquith's second and instructed him to remain in Pennsylvania while he wrote McCullough regarding a face-off to settle the matter. After his demands were ignored or rejected by

McCullough, Aisquith finally returned to Annapolis and his job.

But the feud by now was a matter of detailed news coverage, to the point where a law enforcement officer was dispatched on September 27 to arrest both men. They were brought before a judge who ordered them to pay $2,500 bail each (more than $78,000 in today's currency) as surety against engaging in a duel within the state. The bail for each was posted by influential friends from legal and Democratic party circles, and each attorney returned to business as usual.

EPILOGUE

Spousal homicides were rare throughout the 17th, 18th and 19th centuries in North America. When the victim was a wife, there was a specific name for it, although a name almost never used or heard— uxoricide, from the Latin *uxor* for wife. For some reason, the rate of such crimes increased noticeably in the 1820s and 1830s. In New Hampshire and Vermont, for example, the rate of increase in the late 1820s was fivefold.

Before the Civil War, the weapon of choice for killing one's wife was rarely a gun. According to one study:

> *If the perpetrator was an abusive husband, he clubbed, beat, or stabbed his victim. Perpetrators who had no history of abuse and merely wanted to get rid of their spouses usually drowned, burned, or poisoned them. Nonlethal marital violence had always been a problem, but after the 1820s lethal violence escalated, especially in marriages in which the wife embraced any of the new ideals of sobriety, companionate marriage, and domesticity but the husband did not. Such husbands, nearly all of them poor, alcoholic, and socially isolated, a substantial minority of them*

German, Irish, or French immigrants, brutalized their wives in ways that had been unheard of in colonial and revolutionary times.

Stealth murders of spouses, on the other hand, were the province of respected, native-born Protestants. Their concern with reputation and property made divorce unthinkable. They made the decision to kill out of a desire to improve their lives, to make room for a new lover, or to rid themselves of a spouse they no longer loved.

MODERN TIMES

Globally today, more than 35 percent of all murders of women are reportedly committed by an intimate partner. In fact, available research shows that women are more likely to be killed by a husband, boyfriend, partner or ex than by anyone else. In the last decade, 15 times as many females were murdered by a male they knew than by male strangers. There is often another woman.

Sometimes, it is that woman, the other love interest, who helps to solve the case. Then it is the killer who feels betrayed. The irony defies reason.

ENDNOTES

CHAPTER 1

A BONE–CHILLING BEGINNING

1 ...frozen to crippling depths... The National Weather Service did not put the Wind Chill Equivalent Temperature into regular use until 1973.

1 The thaw finally came... "The End of the Ice Blockade," *The Baltimore Sun*, Jan. 15, 1877, p. 1.

3 At night, the ice breaking against the screwpile piers... "Letter from Annapolis," *The Baltimore Sun*, Jan. 16, 1877, p. 4.

3 ...and its keepers survived... Today, with the addition of a massive icebreaker about 90 feet upstream, and loose stone, or riprap, at its foundation, Thomas Point is one of only 30 lighthouses remaining of the 90 that dotted the Bay 100 years ago, and the only screwpile still in place.

4 Their stock of provisions depleted... "Disasters to Baltimore Oyster Vessels," *The Baltimore Sun*, Jan. 13, 1877, p. 4.

4 Three of the severed schooners... *The Baltimore Sun*, Jan. 13, 1877, p. 4.

5 Meanwhile, on the East River... "The Ice Embargo," *The Baltimore Sun*, Jan. 6, 1877, p. 1.

6 Describing it as the first known passage... "Daring Skating Feat by a Young Lady," *St. Mary's Beacon*, Jan. 18, 1877, p. 4.

A WORLD APART

6 The problem was that as of January 1... "Telegraphic News from Washington," *The Baltimore Sun*, Jan. 8, p. 1.

7 The New Year's reception... "White House in a Blaze of Splendor," *Calvert Journal*, Jan. 13, 1877, p. 1.

9 *The streets were alive...* "Special Dispatch," *Calvert Journal*, Mar. 10, 1877, p. 2.

10 By late fall, the newspaper... Editorial, *Calvert Journal*, Dec. 8, 1877, p. 2.

OUT LIKE A LION

11 The hotel and many of the adjacent cottages... "Fire at Point Lookout," *St. Mary's Beacon*, Mar. 22, 1877, p. 2.

13 The sales price was either... "Sale of Solomon's Island," St. Mary's Beacon, Mar. 22, 1877, p. 2; *The Baltimore Sun*, Mar. 14, 1877, p. 1.

CHAPTER 2

AN UNFORGETTABLE SPRING

20 Around noon, when Henry Norfolk... "Horrible Murder in Anne Arundel County," *The Baltimore Sun*, May 29, 1877, p. 4.

CHAPTER 3

LAYING TO REST

24 The Reverend Sinclair Neal... "Horrible Murder in Anne Arundel County," *The Baltimore Sun*, May 29, 1877, p. 4.

CHAPTER 4

THE INQUEST

27 A few days after Sallie's funeral... "A Young Wife Murdered," *Pittsburgh Post-Gazette*, May 30, 1877, p. 1.

THE EXPERT

33 Other Aiken contributions... *Baltimore Daily Commercial*, Feb. 12, 1868, p. 2.

33 A few years earlier, he had certified... *The Baltimore Sun*, May 5, 1866, p. 2.

33 ...and he gave his scientific thumbs up... *Baltimore Daily Commercial*, Oct. 11, 1865, p. 2.

33   More recently, in the same week... *The Baltimore Sun*, May 30, 1877, p.1.

33   Serving also as a city inspector... *The Baltimore Sun*, Dec. 27, 1882, p. 4.

THE JURY DECIDES

36   Another paper went further... "The Anne Arundel Murder," *The Baltimore Sun*, May 30, 1877, p. 4.

CHAPTER 5

THE ANNAPOLIS JAIL

39   "He talks cheerfully on all subjects..." Letter from Annapolis, *The Baltimore Sun*, July 13, 1877, p. 4.

A RICKETY OLD BUILDING

41   The prisoner quickly found the key... "What a Prisoner Says of Our Jail," *Annapolis Maryland Republican and State Capital Advertiser*, May 17, 1873, p. 3.

THE SIMMS LYNCHING

41   Their actions, reported in detail... "Lynch Law in Anne Arundel Co.," *Star Democrat*, June 22, 1875, p. 2.

41   Referring to the "old rickety building"... "Outrage in Anne Arundel County," *The Baltimore Sun*, June 8,1877, p. 1.

44   The party of masked and disguised men... "Lynch Law in Anne Arundel Co.," *Star Democrat*, June 22, 1875, p. 2.

NO IMPROVEMENT

45   The headline on the newspaper report... "A Weak Old Jail," *The Baltimore Sun*, Feb. 7, 1899, p. 8.

CHAPTER 6

THE SUMMER OF THEIR DISCONTENT

47 The explosion that erupted on the streets... "The Baltimore Railroad Strike and Riot of 1877: Sample Notes from *The Baltimore Sun*," Maryland State Archives: MSA S2221-9-12 Documents.

LOCAL OPTION LAW

50 *We believe that in time...* Editorial, *Calvert Journal*, May 4, 1877, p. 1.

51 Their trials were scheduled... "Letter from Calvert County, Md.," *The Baltimore Sun*, May 12, 1877, p. 12.

52 Every steamboat boasted its own... *Democratic Advocate*, Sept. 8, 1877, p. 4.

53 *This is indeed "hard lines"...* Editorial, *Calvert Journal*, Sept. 1, 1877, p. 1.

CHAPTER 7

GRAND JURY

56 After being in session ten days... "Letter from Annapolis," *The Baltimore Sun*, Oct. 27, 1877, p. 4.

FOUR MURDER INDICTMENTS

57 *He was carefully dressed for the occasion...* "Letter from Annapolis," *The Baltimore Sun*, Oct. 20, 1877, p. 4.

60 A newspaper report... "Letter from Annapolis," *The Baltimore Sun*, Oct. 27, 1877, p. 4.

CHAPTER 8

A DAY AT THE RACES

61 Some 40 miles from Annapolis... "A Day at the Races—In 1877," *The Baltimore Sun*, Oct. 17, 1937, p. SM 9.

65 Many said it was Parole... "Brilliant Performance at Pimlico," *The Baltimore Sun*, Oct. 25, 1877, p. 1.

CHAPTER 9

THE TRIAL

66 The Court ordered attachments... "Letter from Annapolis," *The Baltimore Sun*, Oct. 30, 1877, p. 4.

DAY ONE

67 Richard Drury, postmaster of the village of Friendship... "Trial for Wife Murder," *The Baltimore Sun*, Oct. 31, 1877, p. 4.

68 Cruentation was admissible evidence... "Did You Know that Bleeding Corpses Were Once Used by Courts to Solve Murders?" by William Aird, The Blood Project: www.thebloodproject.com.

DAY TWO

69 First on the stand was Prof. Aiken... "The Norfolk Murder Trial," *The Baltimore Sun*, Nov. 2, 1877, p. 4.

70 The defendant's brother, Benjamin Norfolk... Ibid.

70 She testified that she had seen... Ibid.

72 The court adjourned until the next morning... Ibid.

DAY THREE

72 Then it was Henry Norfolk's turn... "The Norfolk Murder Trial," *The Baltimore Sun*, Nov. 3, 1877, p. 4.

CLOSING ARGUMENTS

78 At 10 o'clock that evening the case... Ibid.

TRAGEDY ON SOLOMON'S ISLAND

78 Solomon's Island was drenched... "Drowning of a Physician on Solomon's Island," *The Baltimore Sun*, Nov. 6, 1877, p. 4.

CHAPTER 10

THE VERDICT

81 On November 3, Sheriff Nutwell escorted the four... "Letter from Annapolis," *The Baltimore Sun*, Nov. 5, 1877, p. 4.

84 He was said to be "completely unnerved"... "Awaiting His Doom," *The Baltimore Sun*, Nov. 6, 1877, p. 4.

CHAPTER 11

THE DEATH SENTENCE

86 A motion for a new trial was made... "Letter from Annapolis: Sentenced to be Hanged," *The Baltimore Sun*, Nov. 13, 1877, p. 4.

A DEATH WARRANT FOR A CONDEMNED MAN

87 *The State of Maryland: To the sheriff...* "The Death Penalty," *The Baltimore Sun*, Nov. 15, 1877, p. 4.

88 This time they found him... "Reading a Death Warrant to a Condemned Man," *The Baltimore Sun*, Nov. 15, 1877, p. 4.

THE GOVERNOR

90 Unless evidence that established such doubt... "A Little Hatchet in Jan.," *The Baltimore Sun*, Nov. 19, 1877, p. 4.

CHAPTER 12

CONVERSION, CONFESSION, BLAME AND FORGIVENESS

93 Annapolis Jail, Dec. 1, 1877—To the Public... "No Reprieve for Henry Norfolk," *The Baltimore Sun*, Dec. 4, 1877, p. 4.

HISTORY ON THE NEWSSTANDS

96 *I left my house 10 minutes before 8...* "The Anne Arundel Wife Murderer: Confession of Henry Norfolk—He Recounts the Story of the Deed," *The Baltimore Sun*, Dec. 12, 1877, p. 1.

99 *The counsel left to me to give or not...* "Letter from Annapolis: Norfolk, the Wife Murderer—Additional Confession," *The Baltimore Sun*, Dec. 13, 1877, p. 4.

JUST AS GUILTY

102 The defamatory letter was published... *Cincinnati Commercial*, Dec. 22, 1877, p. 4.

CHAPTER 13

THE GALLOWS

104 As his day of execution drew nigh... "The Gallows!" *Maryland Republican and State Capital Advertiser*, Dec. 22, 1877, p. 2.

THE FINAL HOURS

105 In 1877, 47 murderers were hanged... "Methodist Church Statistics," *The Baltimore Sun*, Jan. 2, 1878, p. 1.

107 He was reported to be overrun... "Annapolis Annals: A Notable Wedding—That Hanging Bee," *The Washington Post*, Dec. 15, 1877, p.3.

107 While only a limited number... "Henry Norfolk," *Chicago Evening Journal*, Dec. 22, 1877, p. 2.

FIFTEEN STEPS

108 According to one report... "The Gallows," *Staunton (VA) Vindicator*, Dec. 28, 1877, p.2.

REACTION

111 *The annals of our county or State do not show...* "The Gallows!" *Maryland Republican and State Capital Advertiser*, Dec. 22,1877, p. 2.

POSTSCRIPT

116 In early September, 1878, while en route... "Two Belligerent Lawyers," *Lancaster (PA) Intelligencer*, Sept. 25, 1878, p. 2.

116 According to reports at the time... "To Moral Combat," *Beaver Dam (WI) Argus*, Oct. 3, 1878, p. 1.

117 But the feud by now was a matter of detailed news... "They Found Their Man," *The Cincinnati Inquirer*, Sept. 28, 1878, p. 1.

EPILOGUE

118   *If the perpetrator was an abusive husband... American Homicide*, by Randolph Roth (Harvard University Press, 2009), p. 253.

MODERN TIMES

119   Globally today, more than 35%... "Femicide Report," *WHO*, 2012.

119   In fact, available research shows... "Intimate Partner Violence: Attributes of Victimization, 1993–2011," by Shannan Catalano, Ph.D., Bureau of Justice Statistics, National Crime Victimization Survey.

The Farmer's Wife

ACKNOWLEDGMENTS

Many thanks to all who helped pull together this diorama of a wild year in Maryland history. It's hard to imagine 12 months full of so many extremes, from nature to politics, and most stunning of all—human behavior.

I am grateful as always to Fredrica Depew for her keen editorial eye and rock-solid feedback; to Peggy Kingston for superb genealogical research; to Nate Miller, Rhys Burns and Darby Nisbett at the Maryland State Archives; Myles Conway, proprietor of Friendship Antiques; Anne Causey at the Small Special Collections Library, University of Virginia; Laine Gleisner-Ritchey, Registrar, Calvert Marine Museum; John Jewitt, Public Services Librarian, St. John's College, Annapolis; Karen D. Boyd, Cemetery Chairperson, and Marjorie Lewis, Friendship UME Church; Douglas Hofstedt, Court Administrator, Anne Arundel County Circuit Court; and Tara Wink, Historical Collections Librarian and Archivist, University of Maryland. And finally, thanks to Sandra Olivetti Martin, New Bay Books, for always wise counsel, and Suzanne Shelden, an artist who can portray the world through any prism.

I am indebted to all.

—Carol Booker